MW00446900

IT'S JUST F🪷CKING MEDITATION

IT'S JUST F🪷CKING MEDITATION

HOW TO FIND YOURSELF, CALM YOUR ANXIETY & MANIFEST THE LIFE OF YOUR DREAMS

Bryan Holub

Creator of the Relax with Yogi Bryan podcast & certified yoga instructor

PAGE STREET
PUBLISHING CO.

PAGE STREET
PUBLISHING CO.

Copyright © 2023 Bryan Holub

First published in 2023 by
Page Street Publishing Co.
27 Congress Street, Suite 1511
Salem, MA 01970
www.pagestreetpublishing.com

All rights reserved. No part of this book may be reproduced or used, in any form or by any means, electronic or mechanical, without prior permission in writing from the publisher.

Distributed by Macmillan, sales in Canada by The Canadian Manda Group.

27   26   25   24   23   1 2   3 4   5

ISBN-13: 978-1-64567-832-8
ISBN-10: 1-64567-832-6

Library of Congress Control Number: 2022952258

Cover and book design by Emma Hardy for Page Street Publishing Co.
Photography by Nicole Curtin

Printed and bound in the United States

Page Street Publishing protects our planet by donating to nonprofits like The Trustees, which focuses on local land conservation.

DEDICATION

This book is dedicated to my parents, Georg and Maxine;
my brother, Brandon; and my good friend Pratik.
I couldn't have written this book without your support,
thank you so much.

CONTENTS

INTRODUCTION

WELCOME! I'M SO GLAD YOU PICKED UP THIS BOOK. You must be ready to meditate like a *fuckin' pro!* Yes, you heard that right. I'm here to help all you fuckers out there start a meditation practice. Who said meditation had to be all serious and serene? Not me!

This book is written specifically for people who are just starting out with meditation and want to get better at it without becoming bogged down in the seriousness that can sometimes be associated with the practice. This book is for you if you have any interest in meditation at all, whether it be skepticism or curiosity. This is a step-by-step program that will assist you in developing a daily meditation practice that is tailored to your specific needs.

I am aware that beginning a meditation practice, particularly if you are new to the discipline, can be difficult. Because of this, I decided to write this book with straight-up advice and approachable tips in the hope that it may make the process easier for you to handle. You will discover how to meditate, how to overcome common barriers and how to establish a unique meditation practice that is tailored to your lifestyle.

Honestly, I never thought I'd be writing a how-to-meditate book. But, here we are. It all started with a hilarious idea to create an Instagram account to poke fun at yoga. I mean, who doesn't love a good laugh? As I stumbled into the world of yoga, I fell head over heels in love with it. It became my lifeline during a tough time in my life, and it changed me for the better.

It was my yoga practice that introduced me to the world of meditation. One day, I decided to challenge myself and meditate for 90 days straight. Let me tell you, it was pure torture at first. I couldn't sit still for two minutes without fidgeting. But I stuck with it, and after 77 days, something clicked. Meditation became my superpower. It made me more aware of myself and helped me find solutions to problems.

Fast forward to today, and I'm a meditation master. Okay, maybe not a master, but I've meditated pretty much every day since 2019. I even created a guided meditation podcast called *Relax with Yogi Bryan*, which has millions of listens! And now, I've created the *It's Just F*ckin Meditation* podcast and Relax with Yogi Bryan app, all to help the world release unnecessary fucks and chill.

So, my dear reader, whether you're a meditation newbie or a seasoned pro, I hope this book helps you on your journey to becoming more aware of yourself and releasing those fucks. Remember to be gentle with yourself, and let's do this fuckin' thing!

SET

YOUR

INTENTIONS

TIPS FOR READING THIS BOOK

Here are some tips and tricks for how to read this meditation book, so that you can get the most out of the information it contains.

TIP 1: SET YOUR INTENTIONS

Put on your goal-setting hat before you start devouring the pages in this book. Just how do you plan to transform your life thanks to meditation ? Have you set your sights on enlightenment? Achieving some sort of personal serenity? It's time to decide on some goals and prepare for an exciting journey, whatever those goals may be. If you take the time to establish a plan before diving into this book, you will find it more satisfying than eating a plate of warm cookies. Be ready to enjoy the fruits of your reading labor. Take some time to set your intentions for this book right now.

TIP 2: CREATE A COMFORTABLE READING ENVIRONMENT

Okay, fellow fuckers! Find the perfect place to relax and lose yourself in the reading. Choose a place where you can read in peace and quiet, whether it's a comfy couch in the living room or a secluded corner of the backyard. Oh, and make sure your spot is well illuminated and maybe play some groovy tunes to really get the party started. Reading without ambiance and good music is like eating a taco without salsa: completely unacceptable. Relax, open this book and enjoy the ride.

TIP 3: READ SLOWLY AND MINDFULLY

When reading this book, it's important to focus, as much as it is when you meditate. Don't rush through the reading, it's not a fuckin' race; instead, give each page your full attention and make sure you fully understand what's being said. You should keep reading even if you become aware that your mind has wandered; all you have to do is gently concentrate on what you're doing to bring it back to the present moment.

TIP 4: TAKE NOTES AND HIGHLIGHT KEY POINTS

While you are reading, you should make notes and underline any important themes that resonate with you. You will have an easier time remembering the material and incorporating it into your practice of meditation as a result. To keep track of your ideas and realizations, you might want to keep a journal or notebook handy. It really helps.

TIP 5: PRACTICE WHAT YOU LEARN

The most essential step after reading this book about meditation is to put the information you've gained into practice. Do not simply read the information and then put it completely out of your mind. Take ACTION. Integrate the practices and the guiding principles into your day-to-day activities, and make a commitment to beginning and maintaining a regular meditation practice. The more you put what you learn in this book into practice, the more you will profit from what it has to offer.

Reading this book on meditation is a strong tool that can help you improve your meditation practice and your overall well-being if you do it regularly. You may get the most out of this book and take your meditation practice to the next level by setting your objectives, creating an environment that is comfortable for reading, reading deliberately and mindfully, taking notes and marking essential parts, and implementing what you learn. Keep in mind that you should have patience, maintain your concentration and enjoy the ride!

CHAPTER 1

GET YOUR SHIT TOGETHER WITH MEDITATION

OKAY, LOTUS PETALS, FASTEN YOUR SEATBELTS AND GET READY FOR SOME SERIOUS ENLIGHTENMENT! We are going to talk about why meditation is so damn important, and I promise that I won't get all profound and Zen on you during this discussion.

To begin, let's get one thing straight: meditation is not something that is only practiced by hippies, monks or people who have an excessive amount of free time on their hands. You can put your skepticism aside because meditation applies to everyone, including *you*.

You may be wondering why it is that meditation is considered so vital. To begin, it's a wonderful opportunity to relax and unwind, to the fullest extent possible. Let's face it, living life can be stressful at times, and when you start to feel stressed, all you need to do is take a few deep breaths and get your bearings. And what more effective way is there to do that than to simply sit in stillness, concentrate on your breathing and imagine that you are a sage old master?

But hold on, there's more to it! Research has shown that practicing meditation can be beneficial to one's health. That's right, folks: By devoting a short amount of time each day to meditative introspection, you have the potential to improve a variety of aspects of your health, including your blood pressure, anxiety levels and immune function. Meditation functions in the same way as a daily dose of medication, but with none of the unpleasant side effects.

And let's not overlook the positive effects on one's mental health. Meditation, when practiced on a regular basis, can help you maintain focus, improve your memory and enhance your sense of well-being overall. In addition, it is an excellent method of evading the relentless onslaught of notifications, emails and social media updates, all of which have the potential to make you feel as though your head is about to burst.

THE MANY FACES OF MEDITATION

When it comes to meditation, it can be difficult to determine which form of meditation is best for you because there are so many different kinds. It's like trying to pick your favorite flavor of ice cream at Baskin-Robbins® when there are so many different flavors to choose from; there are just too many good options. There are so many different meditation practices to choose from but do not worry, my fellow meditators who are mind-fucked: I am here to assist you.

There is no better way to ease into the practice of meditation than with the age-old method of "sitting meditation." This method of meditation, which has been around for centuries and has several names like "Zen meditation" and "Vipassana," has many benefits. Sitting meditation is a way to cultivate awareness, focus and calmness. Envision yourself in a relaxing chair, perhaps with your legs crossed or propped up on a cushion. Both your eyes and mind are closed while you concentrate on each inhale and exhale. By focusing on your breathing, you'll be able to push out any unwanted ideas or emotions that try to make a home of your mind.

You'd think it would be simple. You're literally simply sitting there and taking in air. Yet, the reality is that sitting meditation is much harder than it appears. A good analogy is trying to catch a butterfly with chopsticks; you might think it's easy—until you try.

You possess a potent tool in your mind, and it enjoys exploring new territory. It's difficult to maintain concentration because your mind is always racing from one idea to the next. But, that is precisely what sitting meditation is meant to do: It will help you calm your mind and find peace even in the middle of chaos by centering the focus on your breath and using your breath as your anchor. The rewards much outweigh the time, effort and frustration involved.

Why not try it then? Take a moment to yourself to sit in relative peace and breathe deeply. Though not always simple, it is unquestionably worthwhile. Catching a butterfly with chopsticks might not be as impossible as you think.

Don't worry if you've given up on sitting motionless and pretending to meditate while your mind wanders off to the land of daydreams and distractions. I'd like to introduce you to "movement meditation," or what I like to call "meditation for individuals who can't sit still."

Don't let the fancy name mislead you. In essence, this just means that you can go about your day at your own pace, without worrying about how others are spending their time. What's more, this form of meditation on the go has some impressive sounding names, like "qigong" or "tai chi." But, have no fear; you won't need a background in ancient Chinese philosophy to give this type of meditation a shot.

As you take a gentle walk, bike or practice your yoga flow, picture yourself floating effortlessly through the air like a gorgeous swan, minus the feathers and the strange honking sounds. You're out in the open air, taking in a healthy dose of oxygen, and your every motion is smooth and easy. It's like dancing, only without the pressure of having to impress someone or the embarrassment of having to dance in front of a complete stranger.

What's even better? The physical exercise is helping your brain as much as your body. It's like getting two benefits for the price of one: You're getting a better state of mind *and* body. In that case, why not give it a shot? The benefits for your body and mind are obvious, and you never know, maybe you'll even find your swan side. You'll have fun while getting some healthy activity, at the very least.

The practice of "mantra meditation," also referred to as "transcendental meditation," is yet another form of meditation. Meditation in which a word or phrase is repeated over and over is called "word repetition meditation." It's kind of like trying to meditate while you're singing karaoke; it's about finding your own inner voice.

Last but not least, there's something called "mindfulness meditation." Meditation on mindfulness is the practice of paying attention to what is happening in the here and now without attaching any value judgments or opinions to that attention. It's like trying to concentrate on the flavor of a piece of chocolate while keeping your thoughts from wandering to all the other things you need to get done later. It should not be that difficult, should it? Yet, in practice, it's a lot harder than it seems.

Consider the situation as if you were attempting to meditate while concurrently watching an episode of your favorite soap opera. You are making an effort to maintain your concentration on the here and now, but your thoughts keep being distracted by the action and excitement that is taking place on the screen.

But, precisely because of this, the practice of mindfulness meditation is so powerful. You can create a sense of peace and clarity that will assist you in dealing with whatever challenges life may give you if you learn to remain present and focused in the moment. You learn to become more aware of your ideas and emotions, without allowing yourself to be dominated by them. You develop a greater awareness of your physical self and a deeper connection to the world around you.

How exactly do you go about practicing mindfulness meditation? It is, in all honesty, not too difficult. This practice is the same as seated meditation; it's just being more present and aware of the present moment. Choose a place where there isn't much noise and you can sit comfortably with your back straight and your eyes closed. Put all of your attention on your breath, and make an effort to let go of any other thoughts or distractions that come to mind. In the event that your mind starts to wander, bring it back to your breath in a gentle and slow manner. The benefits of this routine more than make up for the time and perseverance that it requires to complete it.

Meditation on mindfulness is a practice that can help people achieve serenity and tranquility in a society that is constantly pulling us in a million different directions. It's as if you've pressed the stop button on the craziness that is your typical day, and you've allowed yourself some time to simply be. In that case, why not give it a shot? Who knows, you could find that your favorite soap drama can actually wait 'til later after all.

FINDING YOUR PERFECT MATCH: 'TWAS LOVE AT FIRST OM

How exactly do you determine the type of meditation that best suits your needs? To be honest, it's a matter of trial and error. When it comes to love, it's possible that you'll have to "kiss a few frogs" before you find your true prince (or princess) charming. But you shouldn't worry about it because the process can be enjoyable.

It's possible that you'll find that sitting meditation is your jam, and if so, that's awesome. However, if you find that you are becoming antsy, you should try practicing moving meditation. Mantra meditation is another option to consider if you often find that you are preoccupied with your own thoughts. Try practicing mindfulness meditation if you often find that your thoughts are wandering to the past or the future.

The practice of meditation, much like a personal connection, can develop and evolve over time. And that is perfectly fine. Your meditation practice will change and develop as you go through life's ups and downs.

Finding the right method of meditation can feel like a journey at times, but don't let that deter you. Keep in mind that meditating is more of a process than an end goal. And just like any other form of practice, making sure you have fun while doing it is essential. Take a deep breath, grab some chopsticks, some dancing shoes, a microphone and your favorite soap opera, and let's meditate, you fuckers.

BENEFITS OF MEDITATION

We are going to delve into the scientific aspects of meditation, so make sure you have your crystals and your yoga pants ready. Believe me when I say that this information is supported by more studies than you could possibly poke a stick at.

Shall we begin with the state of your mental health? A study that was published in the journal *Neuropsychobiology* found that practicing mindfulness meditation can help reduce symptoms of mental health conditions such as anxiety and depression. Even if you don't struggle with an anxiety disorder or depression, everyone deals with tough emotions from time to time. So the next time Fred in Accounting is driving you absolutely bonkers, simply take a few deep breaths and try to picture him as a tranquil flower. This should help. I swear that it is effective.

But hold on, there's more to it! Your body can benefit tremendously from the practice of meditation as well. A study that was conducted at the Harvard Medical School found that regular meditation can help lower blood pressure and even boost your immune system. Pretty cool stuff, right?

And, fucker, let's not overlook manifestation! Meditation on loving-kindness, as described in a recent article published in the *Annual Review of Clinical Psychology*, has been shown to help increase positive emotions as well as social connections. So, the next time you find yourself feeling isolated, try visualizing yourself amidst a throng of adoring fans. It should help. It's a lot like *The Secret*, but there's less of a focus on the supernatural and more on the science.

MEDITATION MYTHS BUSTED

Oh, the meditative state. Meditation has been around for centuries, but for some reason it still manages to be shrouded in mystery and misconceptions. Therefore, shall we set the record straight? The following are some of the most widespread misunderstandings regarding meditation:

Misconception #1: You Have to Be Religious or Spiritual to Meditate

Wrong, wrong, wrong. Although meditation has its origins in various religious and spiritual practices, to experience its benefits, you are not required to have any particular belief system. It doesn't matter if you believe in anything or not; what matters is that you learn to embrace your thoughts and focus on the here and now.

Misconception #2: Meditation Is Only for People Who Are Really Good at It

Au contraire, my friend. Because it is a practice, meditation is something that requires consistent effort over the course of its use. Believe me when I say that no one starts out as a Zen master. If you're having trouble calming your mind or concentrating on your breathing, don't give up; just keep practicing. The more you do it, the simpler it will become.

Misconception #3: You Have to Sit Cross-Legged on the Floor to Meditate

Although this is a common image of meditation, sitting quietly like this is not the only way to meditate. It is possible to practice meditation while sitting in a chair, lying down or even walking. Finding a comfortable position that enables you to concentrate on your breath while also allowing you to clear your mind is the most important thing.

Misconception #4: Meditation Is a Waste of Time

If you believe that it is a waste of time to take a few minutes out of your day to relax your mind and lower your levels of stress, then I don't know what to say to you. But the fact of the matter is that meditating has been shown by various scientific studies to have several mental and physical health benefits. Therefore, if you are looking for a way to improve your well-being and you think that meditation might be the answer, you should give it a try.

Misconception #5: Meditation Is Easy and Anyone Can Do It

Although in theory, anyone is capable of meditating, in practice it can be challenging. When you're just starting out, it can be particularly difficult to still your thoughts and concentrate on your breathing without letting your mind wander. But don't let that discourage you! You will become better at it with time and practice, and you will begin to see the benefits of doing so.

Meditation is not a cure, but it may be a very useful technique in helping you develop a stronger sense of inner calm, clarity and concentration in your life and on your goals. It is a method for ensuring that you are not merely surviving in life, but thriving in it as well.

So, why not give it a shot? It is not necessary to begin your meditation practice with a 2-hour session each day, as some of the more dedicated practitioners recommend. You should aim to practice every day, even if it's for just a few minutes at first, and then progressively increase the amount of time you spend meditating.

It is important to keep in mind that there is no one best approach to meditating. Pick a method that serves you well, and don't be hesitant to try out several approaches until you discover something that strikes a chord with you.

And, as a final piece of advice, try not to take it too seriously! The practice of meditation ought to be something exciting and pleasurable to do. If you're not enjoying yourself, then what the fuck are you doing? Now, relax, draw a big breath and let's embark on this adventure of self-discovery together. Let your hair down and take a moment to center yourself.

CHAPTER 2

THE STRUGGLE BUS— WHY YOU CAN'T FUCKIN' MEDITATE

FINDING STILLNESS AND CALMNESS WITHIN ONESELF is the goal of the practice of meditation, but let's be honest: It's not always easy to get there. There are times when life simply gets in the way.

THE EXCUSES

In this chapter, we will discuss the many reasons why people are unable to meditate, and we will also provide some solutions for those individuals who just can't seem to find their zen.

I Can't Sit Still!

The very thought of remaining motionless and doing nothing for even a short period of time can be excruciatingly painful for certain individuals. The moment that person closes their eyes, their mind immediately begins to race with a multitude of thoughts. They begin to shift in their seats and wriggle around, and before they realize it, they are sitting upright and using their phone again. To meditate, however, you need not remain seated for the duration of the practice. You might give walking meditation, yoga or any other practice a shot if you're looking for something that will help you concentrate your thoughts and discover a sense of inner peace.

I Can't Stop Thinking!

Another issue that frequently arises for people who are new to meditation is an inability to calm the mind. The moment they close their eyes, their brain enters a state of hyperactivity. They dwell on the day's events at work, including the awkward exchange they had with a coworker or the tasks on their to-do list. But, that is to be expected. The important thing is to recognize that you're having those thoughts and then to let them go. You shouldn't bother trying to fight them; instead, you should just let them come and go. Try visualizing yourself taking a step back to the bank and letting thoughts flow by in a stream rather than swimming in the current yourself. In addition, keep in mind that the more you practice, the simpler it will be for you to still your mind.

I Don't Have Time!

It can be difficult to make time for meditation when one has to balance the demands of work, family and other commitments. However, here's the thing: To meditate, you don't need a lot of time at all. Even if you only spend 5 minutes a day on your practice, you can see results. Try getting up a little bit earlier, taking a 5-minute break while you're at work or meditating right before you go to sleep. You won't believe how much of a change can come from just a few minutes' worth of your time.

I Can't Find the Right Place!

When it comes to meditation, some people think it requires the ideal setting: total silence, the appropriate amount of light and the optimal temperature. Instead of searching for the "ideal" setting, you should search for the ideal setting for you personally. Try meditating during your lunch break or while you are waiting for your children to finish their soccer practice. When you put in the effort to practice in a variety of settings, finding your inner sanctuary will become easier and easier, regardless of where you are.

I Don't Know How!

There are some people who find the concept of meditation completely foreign. They have no idea how to begin, what they should do or where to even begin looking for answers. The good news is that you will learn how to meditate by reading this book. You shouldn't let your anxiety about the future prevent you from finding your inner peace. Take a few slow, deep breaths and leap right in.

In the end, the most important thing to remember about meditation is that you shouldn't take it too seriously. It is acceptable for life to be a jumbled, chaotic and hilarious mess. Accept the disorder, admit that you have excuses and keep working on your skills. It won't be long before you start discovering a sense of calm and contentment in the strangest of places, and that's wonderful.

FINDING THE PERFECT SPOT

Finding inner peace in meditation can be challenging to accomplish when one is surrounded by a chaotic environment. Therefore, it is essential to find the appropriate location and atmosphere that will be conducive to your success. There isn't a singular perfect spot; different spaces can serve perfectly at different times in the day. In this section we will discuss some helpful hints on how to find the ideal location for meditation without driving yourself crazy.

Look for the Quiet Spaces

Look for places with a lot of peace and quiet if you want to find a good spot for meditation. This could be an unused bedroom, a peaceful nook in your living room or even a storage space in your home. My meditation spot is right next to my bed, with a comfy meditation cushion to sit on. The most important thing is to find a location where you can be by yourself and unbothered for a chunk of time. And if you have to get a little creative with the location, that's totally fine. Make sure that it is a place where you can unwind and concentrate on the task at hand.

Make It Your Own

After you have found the ideal location, it is fun to personalize it in some way, but no need to overthink it. Candles, incense and other meditative implements could be used as part of the room's decor to achieve this effect. It's also possible that all that's required is a pillow or cushion on the floor. Do whatever it is that puts you at ease and helps you feel comfortable. And if that means keeping your pet dog or cat close by, then by all means, do it. They are capable of being wonderful meditation partners unless they keep putting their nose in your butt.

Don't Be Afraid to Experiment

First time around isn't always the charm for everyone when it comes to finding the ideal spot to practice meditation. Finding out what works best for you might require some trial and error on your part. Experiment with meditating in various locations throughout your home or even outside your home. It's possible that you'll decide that the great outdoors or a specific room in the house is your favored environment rather than the spot you originally designated. Don't be afraid to use your imagination and try out different approaches until you find what works best for you.

Be Prepared for the Unexpected

Unanticipated sounds or disturbances have the potential to throw even the most well-prepared meditation session off track. As a result, it is critical to ensure that one is ready for anything that may arise. To help block out any potential interruptions, keep a set of headphones with active noise cancellation close at hand, or consider purchasing a white noise machine. If all else fails, just give in to the chaos and try to concentrate on your breathing instead. Use the sounds as a part of your meditation and just be aware they are there. Embrace that jackhammer or the noisy birds outside because you are exactly where you need to be.

At the end of the day, it is essential to keep in mind that the location and atmosphere in which you practice meditation are only a small part of the whole picture. The real challenge lies in adjusting your mental approach. Therefore, whether you are practicing meditation in a calm room or a busy coffee shop, bring your attention to your breathing, acknowledge the thoughts that arise and then let them go. It doesn't matter where you are; what matters most is that you find that inner peace.

Finding the ideal spot in which to meditate can be difficult at times, but the pursuit of this goal does not have to drive you crazy. Find places with some peace and quiet, personalize the environment and be ready for the unexpected. And last but not least, keep in mind that the most important factor is your mental attitude. Accept the disorder, acknowledge the presence of your thoughts and focus on your breathing.

GETTING COMFORTABLE AS FUCK

So, you've made the decision to begin practicing meditation. That's fantastic! But here's the thing: If you're not feeling good about yourself, you're not going to go very far. In addition, if you're anything like me, finding a comfortable position can be a little bit of a struggle. In this section, we'll take a lighthearted approach to discussing some helpful hints on how to set up a comfortable environment for meditation.

The Right Gear

First things first, you're going to need the appropriate equipment. And by gear, I mean clothes that are comfortable. Therefore, pull on your most comfortable pair of sweatpants, and if you are currently wearing a bra, remove it immediately before proceeding. Let those titties be free.

The Perfect Seat

After you've ensured that you're wearing comfortable clothing, it's time to locate the ideal place to sit. But where do we even begin? It's possible that you're an old-fashioned person who likes to sit on the floor with your legs crossed. It's also possible that you're a free spirit who enjoys lounging on a bed or sofa. Whatever your preference, just make sure that your posture isn't throwing you off or distracting you in any way. We will get to posture later in this book; for now, just find a comfortable seat or chair.

Cushions, Pillows and Blankets, Oh My!

To achieve the desired level of coziness, it might be necessary to cover yourself in a thick layer of cushions, pillows and blankets. Don't be afraid to give it your all in this situation. It's possible that your back could use some support from a few pillows, and a warm blanket would help you get cozy. More cushions are always a welcome addition.

Music, Noise or Silence?

When it comes to meditation, some people find that the complete absence of sound is most beneficial, while others favor the accompaniment of gentle music or even white noise. Find out what works best for you, and then stick with that. And if that means turning up some Enya at full volume, then who am I to judge?

Stretch It Out

Take a few minutes to stretch out your body before getting into the position that you find most comfortable. It's possible that you just need to stretch your legs or loosen up your neck. Do not be afraid to experiment with some strange approaches. After all, you're already wearing sweatpants.

Breathe and Relax

Now that everything is ready to go and you've got it all set up, you can take a deep breath and kick back and relax. Put your attention on your breathing while you close your eyes and watch the rest of the world dissolve away. And if you find that you are becoming distracted by how comfortable you are, that is perfectly acceptable. Just notice it and move on.

When it comes to meditation, finding a comfortable position to sit in can be a bit of a challenge, especially for someone as high maintenance as I am. You will, however, be able to find a way to get comfortable if you look for the appropriate gear, locate the ideal seat and then pile on the cushions. And most importantly, do not forget to relax and focus on your breathing.

FINDING TIME TO MEDITATE (BETWEEN NAPS AND SNACKS)

We'd all like to be the kind of people who can meditate each and every day, but let's face it: Life has a way of getting in the way of our best-laid plans. We're pressed for time, under a lot of stress and completely worn out. But have no fear, those of you who put off practicing meditation! I will provide you with some suggestions on how to find time to meditate, even when it appears that there are only 10 seconds left in the day.

The Early Bird Gets the Meditation

Finding a time that is convenient for you should be your first order of business. Perhaps you are someone who enjoys getting up before the sun rises because you are an early riser. You could also be a night owl who practices meditation right before going to bed. It doesn't matter what time you choose, just make sure it's not when you're already feeling sleepy and you'll be fine.

Multitasking Is Key

When you're really pressed for time, the best way to get things done is to multi-task. It's possible that you could practice meditation while you're in the shower or while you're brushing your teeth. Alternately, you could give meditating on your daily commute a shot. Just make sure that you don't miss your stop, unless you really feel like you need that additional time to meditate.

Sneak It In

There are times when you simply have to squeak in some time for meditation. Perhaps you could practice meditation while you are waiting for the laundry to be done or during your lunch break—or even while you're waiting in line at the grocery store. When all else fails, use your imagination. It's possible that you could practice meditation while you're doing your chores, such as cleaning the house or folding the laundry. You could try meditating while you wait for your coffee to brew and smell the great aroma of waking the fuck up.

Remember, It's All About Prioritizing

At the end of the day, everything comes down to setting priorities. Even though we are incredibly busy and have a million things to do, it is still beneficial to take some time out of our day to meditate. Therefore, make it a priority, and keep in mind that there is always time for a brief session of meditation, even if you have to squeeze it in between much-needed naps and snacks.

Finding the time to sit still and reflect through meditation can be difficult at times, particularly when one is overworked and exhausted. And you can find a way to meditate even when it seems impossible if you find a time of day that is convenient for you, multitask, sneak it in and use your imagination. And most importantly, don't forget to make meditation a priority, because taking care of yourself is essential, and you have earned those 10 minutes of calm and solitude.

CLEARING YOUR MIND (OR AT LEAST TRYING TO)

The process of emptying your mind during meditation is one of the more difficult aspects of the practice. Everyone has thoughts racing through their mind at all times, and it may seem impossible to stop them. But do not be afraid, my fellow overthinkers! I will provide you with some suggestions on how to clear your mind during meditation, or at least give it my best effort.

Acknowledge Your Thoughts (But Don't Let Them Take Over)

Recognizing the thoughts that are running through your head is the first step toward mental clarity. It's fine to have thoughts, but you don't have to give in to their demands and let them run your life. Try imagining your thoughts as clouds moving through the sky, and just observe them without passing judgment on what you see. If a thought does spiral you out of the present moment just bring your awareness and attention back to your breathing. Use your breath as your foundation.

Focus on Your Breath (Unless You're Hungry)

One time-honored technique for calming the mind is to concentrate on one's breathing. You can count your breaths, or you just focus on the feeling of air entering and exiting your body as you breathe. However, if you are starving, this is probably not the best choice for you. If that's the case, you should try to concentrate instead on the rumbling in your stomach.

Use Guided Meditations (or Create Your Own)

Clearing your mind can be accomplished quite effectively through the practice of guided meditation. You can choose to do a meditation that is guided, or you can write your own script that will help you unwind and let go of your thoughts. Just make sure you don't nod off unintentionally unless you want to clear your head while dreaming about going on a beach vacation.

Get Physical (in a Non-Violent Way)

Moving your body can sometimes be a good way to help clear your mind. Before you begin to meditate, you might find it helpful to warm up with some light stretching or some yoga poses. You could also go for a short walk or do some jumping jacks if you're feeling particularly antsy and fidgety. Just keep an eye out for anything or anyone that might get in your way during the process.

Accept That Your Mind Might Not Be 100% Clear (and That's Okay)

Accepting that your mind may not be completely clear during meditation is essential if you want to get the most out of the practice. It is perfectly normal to be distracted by thoughts and other things, and the more you practice, the simpler it will be to let go of those thoughts and distractions. And if all else fails, just laugh it off and accept the chaos as your new normal.

STICKING WITH MEDITATION (WITHOUT STICKING YOUR HEAD IN THE SAND)

You must be congratulated on beginning your meditation practice. But now comes the challenging part: maintaining your resolve. It's easy to get pumped up about a new routine, but that excitement can quickly fade after a few days or weeks. But have no fear, other people who are afraid of making commitments! I will offer you some advice on how to maintain your meditation practice without feeling as though you are giving up your mental health in the process.

Make It a Habit (or a Guilty Pleasure)

Making meditation a regular part of your routine is essential to maintaining your practice over time. If you want to get the most out of your meditation sessions, establish a regular time and location for them, and don't let anything get in the way of them. Find a way to make meditation more like a reward for yourself, rather than a task that you have to complete.

Find an Accountability Buddy (or a Supportive Pet)

If you want to maintain your meditation practice, it can be helpful to have someone (or something) to keep you accountable for doing it. Find another person in your life who meditates, whether it be a friend or family member, and make a pact with them to keep each other motivated. Or, find a furry friend to sit with you while you practice if you're more of a dog or cat person.

Mix It Up (but Not Too Much)

The practice of meditation is similar to life in that it benefits from having a variety of approaches. Experiment with various meditative practices, such as body scans, guided meditations and mindfulness exercises. But, be careful not to make too many changes at once, or you risk becoming overwhelmed and giving up entirely.

Celebrate Small Wins (or Just Give Yourself a High Five)

Don't forget to celebrate even the smallest of your victories along the way. It's possible that you were able to detach yourself from your thoughts for an extra 3 minutes, giving you a total of 5, or that you became aware of a slight shift in your disposition. Give yourself a high five or a pat on the back if you're really feeling pumped up about what you've accomplished.

Let Go of Expectations (and Embrace Imperfection)

Last but not least, you should let go of any expectations you have for your meditation practice. This is extremely important. It is not necessary for you to have a mind-blowing realization each time you sit down to meditate. It is not a problem if your thoughts wander or if you become distracted. Accept the fact that you are not perfect and keep in mind that the practice of meditating itself is more important than the results of one session.

You can keep your meditation practice going strong by making it a habit or a guilty pleasure, finding an accountability buddy or supportive pet, mixing it up (but not too much), celebrating small wins, letting go of expectations and embracing imperfection. Also, keep a healthy sense of humor, because having a good laugh is often the most effective way to continue doing something.

OVERCOMING DISTRACTIONS (OR HOW TO MEDITATE WHEN YOUR MIND IS A CIRCUS)

Oh yeah, I've been meditating. The blissful act of sitting in stillness and silence while allowing your mind to wander to more pleasant places, such as what to have for dinner or something embarrassing you did when you were in third grade. It's a wonderful creation all around. But how can we get past these distractions so that we can actually find some peace while we practice? Do not be alarmed, fellow meditators who are easily sidetracked, we will take a lighthearted approach to discussing some strategies for overcoming distractions.

Acknowledge the Distraction (or Name It and Claim It)

Recognizing the existence of the distractions is the first step in removing them. When a thought occurs to you, rather than getting caught up in it or becoming preoccupied by it, try to simply observe it and acknowledge it when it arises. Or, if the thought is particularly bothersome, you can give it a name and assert ownership over it, such as "Good to see you again, Mr. What-If-I-Forgot-to-Turn-Off-the-Stove."

Refocus with Breath (or Hasta La Vista, Distractions)

When you become aware that you are becoming distracted, direct your attention to your breathing. Make a conscious effort to bring your attention back to the here and now by focusing on the feeling of breathing in and out. Or, if you are in the mood for something more dramatic, imagine yourself telling your distractions "hasta la vista, baby" as you refocus your attention on your breath.

Embrace Imperfection (or Roll with the Distractions)

Keep in mind that distractions are an inevitable part of the meditation process. It is normal for your mind to wander, and it's not a problem if you find that certain thoughts won't leave your head. You should make an effort to accept imperfection and learn to roll with distractions. You could even find that some of the things that are distracting you lead to interesting insights or revelations if you give them enough time.

Find Humor in the Distractions (or Make Them Your BFFs)

Don't be afraid to laugh at the things that are distracting you. You might find it helpful to picture your thoughts as the characters in a sitcom, or even to give them humorous voices. Or, if nothing else works, make your interruptions your new best friends forever. You should give them names, carry on conversations with them and incorporate those exchanges into your meditation practice.

The practice of meditation, much like life in general, is not exempt from the presence of distractions. However, if you acknowledge the distractions, refocus with breath, accept imperfection as a part of the practice and find humor in the distractions, you can overcome them and find some peace in your practice. Remember that laughter is the best medicine there is at all times, even when you are in the middle of a meditation practice. When your mind is acting like a circus, the best thing to do is to just relax and enjoy the show.

DON'T BE AN ASSHOLE

DON'T BE AN ASSHOLE

DON'T BE AN ASSHOLE

DON'T BE AN ASSHOLE

DON'T BE AN ASSHOLE

CHAPTER 3

LOVE THYSELF—
ON NOT BEING AN ASSHOLE

THE TIME HAS COME TO TALK ABOUT THE MAGICAL POWER OF HAVING COMPASSION FOR ONESELF. That's right, it's time to put down the whip and pick up the self-love pillow instead.

Now, I'm going to guess what you're thinking. "Bryan, isn't it true that self-compassion is reserved for weaklings?" No brochacho. Self-compassion is for tough individuals who are aware that being kind to themselves is actually the most powerful power move there is.

Just give it some thought. If you are constantly berating yourself for even the smallest of errors, you are doing nothing more than draining your own energy. It's as if you're a bucket of positivity that's always dripping, and every time you criticize yourself, you poke another hole in the bottom of the bucket. However, when you engage in self-compassion practices, you are filling that bucket with some good old-fashioned self-love, fucker.

And here's the kicker: When you are full to the brim with self-love, you are better equipped to handle the problems that life throws at you. It's almost as if you're wearing a suit of armor built of compassion for yourself, which will protect you from the blows that fortune deals you.

So, what exactly does it mean to have compassion for oneself? Actually, compassion can be expressed in a variety of ways. It's possible that you converse with yourself in the same manner that you would with a good friend. You might allow yourself the freedom to err and grow from those experiences. When you're feeling overwhelmed, perhaps you give yourself a break rather than continuing to push yourself to the point of exhaustion.

Realizing that having compassion for oneself does not equate to being weak is a crucial step. It's not about absolving yourself of responsibility or coming up with excuses. It's recognizing that you're a human being and that you're trying your best in every situation. And let's face it, all of our lives could use a little bit more of that kind of thing.

HOW SELF-TALK AFFECTS MENTAL HEALTH

Are you sick and tired of having the recurring feeling that you are your own worst enemy? Do you have the habit of berating yourself for every mistake you make, regardless of how trivial the error may be? Pay attention, because today we are going to talk about how to resist the nasty little negative self-talk creature that dwells in your brain. When you're overly critical of yourself, it's similar to the heightened state of a child who has just watched a scary movie—your brain becomes highly agitated.

Negative self-talk can have some pretty damaging impacts. Negative-self talk has been found to "feed" anxiety and depression, causing an increase in stress levels while lowering levels of self-esteem.

So, what can you do to combat negative self-talk? You have, above all else, a responsibility to recognize when it is occurring. Pay attention to the things you are telling yourself and consider whether you would say those things to a close confidant or friend. Because you're not a jerk, it's highly unlikely that you would do something like that. So why say it to yourself?

After you've become aware of your negative internal dialogue, it's time to start challenging it. Instead of telling yourself, "I'm such an idiot for forgetting my keys," try rephrasing as, "Forgetting my keys was a mistake, but it does not define me as a person."

I am aware that this is easier said than done. Negative self-talk can be a tough habit to break. But the good news is that with practice, you can start to shift your self-talk to be more positive and supportive. And who knows, maybe one day you'll even start to like that voice in your head.

Don't let the mean little voice in your head ruin your life. Challenge it, reframe it and be kind to yourself. You deserve it.

Treat Yourself Like You Would Treat Your Bestie

You know how you always go above and beyond to make your best friend feel as good as possible? Now it is time for you to do the same for yourself, so get to it! Tell yourself, "I'm not going to beat myself up over that pint of ice cream that I just ate," rather than mentally berating yourself over a tasty treat. "You truly do deserve this, girl. You put in a lot of effort today. In addition to that, it contains calcium, so in a scientific sense, it's healthy for you."

Embrace Your Inner Weirdo

Many of us go to great lengths to conceal our individual quirks and idiosyncrasies from those around us. However, your differences make you truly unique. Do yourself a favor and crank on your favorite Taylor Swift tune, then dance crazily around the living room. You know, there's a good reason why her song is titled "Shake It Off."

Give Yourself a Pep Talk

We've all been through those times when we think to ourselves that we just aren't cut out for this world. However, rather than letting that critical voice in your head take control, channel the motivational speaker that lives inside of you. Say to yourself while you're looking in the mirror, "You nailed it like a champ. You are as famous as a rockstar. You are unstoppable by any means." You will earn extra credit if you conclude your response with a cheesy thumbs up.

Take a Break

Due to the hectic nature of our lives, we frequently fail to remember to take some time to unwind and refresh ourselves. Therefore, grant yourself the opportunity to take a break. You could watch multiple episodes of your favorite show in a row, take a nap or read a book. And you should not for one second allow yourself to feel bad about taking some time off. It's called self-care.

It doesn't have to be a tedious chore to practice self-kindness and compassion. Embrace the goofball that exists within you, and treat yourself like the incredible human being that you are. And if all else fails, just remember the sage advice from the *Parks and Rec* TV show: "Treat yo' self."

THE POWER OF GRATITUDE—IT'S OHHH SO SWEET

Harnessing the strength that results from being grateful! What a brilliant concept. You're certainly familiar with the proverb that says a little gratitude can go a long way. And I don't just mean trying to make your mother-in-law feel better by thanking her for the absolutely atrocious sweater she gave you for the holidays.

When it comes to one's mental health, gratitude is actually a superpower. It is comparable to a mystical elixir that has the power to alter one's entire perspective on life. Put down the Xanax and Start being thankful for what you have, baby!

Permit me to explain this to you in more detail. Dopamine and serotonin levels rise, along with other feel-good neurotransmitters, in a person's brain when they are experiencing feelings of gratitude. It's almost like you're having a small rave in your head, and all of your friends are invited. All of a sudden, you become more aware of the many positive aspects of your life, regardless of how trivial or inconsequential they may appear.

This morning at five o'clock, did your neighbor's dog make any noise? No? Thank the hound! Today, did not one of your coworkers prepare fish in the microwave in the office kitchen? Give 'em a big ol' hug! Did you manage to get through the day without getting any coffee on that white shirt you were wearing? Start your joyful dance right now!

However, experiencing a warm and fuzzy sensation on the inside is not the only benefit to gratitude. Being grateful can also help you reframe difficult experiences in a more positive light. You remember that time when your high school sweetheart broke up with you, and you cried yourself to sleep every night for a whole month? You're right, that was a pain. But, you improved as a result. You evolved as a result. And, you most likely now have a killer Spotify playlist to show for it.

Therefore, my dear friends, the power of gratitude should not be undervalued at any cost. It has the power to flip your frown on its head, transform a bad day into a good one and elevate an average life into an extraordinary one. So go ahead and do it: Give thanks even for the insignificant things. And if all else fails, just remember to count your blessings that you're not a cat that got caught in a tree. I'll drink to that!

CHAPTER 4

SIT YOUR ASS DOWN— THE ART OF POSTURE

WHEN IT COMES TO GETTING THE MOST OUT OF YOUR MEDITATIVE EXPERI-ENCE, maintaining proper posture is one of the most important factors. In this chapter, we are going to talk about the necessity of maintaining correct posture and selecting a comfortable position that is suited to your body.

While sitting in meditation, maintaining correct posture can help improve spinal alignment, hence minimizing the likelihood of experiencing pain or discomfort. On the other hand, sitting in one position for a long time can be tedious, which is why it is crucial to establish a posture that is comfortable for you. Because not all positions are created equal, you will need to do some experimenting before you settle on the one that is most comfortable for you.

SITTING LIKE A BOSS

When it comes to sitting still for meditation, having good posture is essential to getting the most out of the experience. And if you're going to spend all that time being sedentary, you might as well do it in style, right?

First, let's discuss the importance of proper posture when it comes to the health benefits of meditation. A study that was published in the journal *Pain Medicine* found that sitting in the correct posture while meditating can help improve spinal alignment, which in turn can help reduce pain and discomfort. Therefore, not only will you be able to meditate like a seasoned professional, you will also be able to sit like one.

It is essential to find not only a proper posture, but one that is comfortable *for you*. Not every posture will work for every body, much like Goldilocks and the three bears in the story. You might find that some are too stiff, while others are too pliable, but with a little trial and error, you'll find the one that's just right for you and your body.

MEDITATION POSTURES: BECAUSE WHO NEEDS A CHIROPRACTOR WHEN YOU CAN JUST SIT AWKWARDLY FOR HOURS

Let's start with the "easy pose" and it is so called because if it weren't easy, it wouldn't be called that. Sitting with your legs crossed and your arms resting on your knees is the basic position for this posture. Doesn't that sound straightforward enough? Well, not so fast.

To begin, you will need to physically assume the cross-legged position on the floor. If you're anything like I was when I first started out, your legs have never even been in the same city, let alone crossed over each other. But don't worry, there is a solution; just elevate your hips by using a cushion or a folded blanket to make it easier to maintain a straight spine. Voila, instant cross-legged success!

Also, check that your hands are resting properly on your knees, meaning that they are not too far in front of or behind you. Keep your spine upright and boom, there you have it. The easy pose is an excellent posture for beginners to practice.

The "seated forward bend" is another common posture, or as I like to refer to it, the "I dropped my keys and can't reach them" position. You will achieve this position by sitting on the ground with your legs stretched out in front of you. Then, you will bend forward as far as you can and attempt to touch your toes.

Now, I don't know how you feel about this, but as far as I'm concerned, my toes might as well be on the Moon for all the chance there is of me reaching them. My hamstrings feel like they are made of steel cables, while the rest of my body feels like it is made of concrete. If I ever find myself in a situation where I need to pick something up off the ground, I just force myself to accept the fact that the object is lost to me.

But I'm getting off topic; let's get back to talking about the posture. The seated forward bend is supposed to help you stretch out your hamstrings and lower back, but all it does for me is make me feel like I have an acceptable reason to go take a nap. I mean, come on, who wouldn't want to roll up into a little ball with their head resting on their knees and catch some z's?

In all seriousness, the seated forward bend is a fantastic exercise for relieving stress and calming the mind because it stretches the front of the body more than the back. Just make sure you don't get too comfortable and end up sleeping through your entire meditation session.

The "chair" is widely considered to be the most accessible and effective posture for meditation. Meditation practiced while seated in a chair is akin to offering the tight hip fuckers a path to enlightenment. Those individuals who simply are unable or unwilling to contort their bodies into unusual shapes will find this pose ideal.

So how do you do it? It's very easy: Locate a chair with a straight back and sit down in it. But hold on, don't make yourself too at home just yet. It is imperative that you ensure that both of your feet are firmly planted on the ground and that your hands are comfortably positioned on either your lap or your knees. In addition, make sure you are sitting up straight because slouching is a habit of amateurs.

If you want to take things to the next level of comfort, you could even try sitting on a meditation cushion instead of the cushion that came with your chair. A meditation cushion sounds like a much better investment than a La-Z-Boy®, doesn't it?

Sitting on a chair while meditating is a great option for people who are just looking for something more comfortable, for people who are just starting out or for anyone who has mobility issues. It is a wonderful way to begin your meditation practice without having to worry about difficult postures or awkward positions. Your enlightenment is waiting for you, so don't be shy; take a seat.

"Savasana" or "corpse pose" is the deepest possible state of relaxation. It's like meditating for the same amount of time as taking a nap, but with more conscious breathing and fewer drool marks.

In savasana, the practitioner lies on their back with their arms and legs extended in front of them with their palms on either side facing downward or upward. The practitioner then allows themselves to melt into the floor. It's like being a human pancake, except that instead of being covered in maple syrup, you are covered in relaxation and inner peace.

Now, I know what you're thinking: "Hold on a second, isn't this just lying down? How exactly does one meditate in this position?" Here's the thing: savasana is more than just a short nap in a comfortable position. In savasana, you can relax and let go of any tension or stress, whether it be mental or physical. Simply be in the moment and let the worries of the outside world melt the fuck away.

And let's not forget the best part: you get to wrap yourself in a warm blanket while you're in this pose! It's as if the universe is giving you a big, warm hug.

All joking aside, the savasana pose is an essential component of any meditation routine. It enables you to fully integrate and absorb the benefits of your meditation session, as well as to connect with the part of yourself that is most fundamental. If you can lie down after your meditation it's like adding a cherry

on top, but it's not required. Your mind, body and spirit will all be better off as a result of your decision to simply lie down and do nothing for a while.

So, to review: To get the most out of your meditation session, it's important to choose the correct position. The advantages of good posture and the possible discomfort of prolonged inactivity must both be taken into account. Common meditation positions include the seated forward bend, the easy pose, the chair and savasana. Each posture has benefits and drawbacks, and it is up to you to choose the one that suits you the best. Finding a comfortable posture and paying attention to your body are essential for a successful meditation session. Keep in mind that the goal is to connect with your more evolved self and experience inner calmness rather than to appear like a seasoned professional. Everyone can sit like a boss and get the most out of meditation with a little trial and error.

BREATHE IN

BREATHE OUT

CHAPTER 5

BREATHE, FUCKER— MASTERING THE BREATH

EVERY SINGLE DAY, WE TAKE APPROXIMATELY 20,000 BREATHS. Isn't that completely insane? It is a staggering number, but most of the time we don't give it much thought. Even though it seems like taking that many breaths should be exhausting us, here we are, breathing without even thinking about it.

The fact of the matter is that breathing is not merely an unconscious process that takes place without any participation on our part. It's not just one system in the body working to keep us alive and healthy; it's actually a complex interplay of different systems in the body—the muscles in our diaphragm, our lungs, our heart and our blood vessels—contributing in some way to the act of breathing.

However, despite the significance of it, we frequently take breathing for granted. We fail to recognize our breath as a constant companion, a constant reminder of the fact that we are alive and connected to the world that surrounds us. If only we could learn to pay attention to our breath, it could serve as a source of strength, of calm and of clarity.

Therefore, let's take a moment to do that very thing. Focus your attention on the breath you are taking right now. (Yes, right now.) Take note of the sensation of air moving in and out of your nostrils as you inhale and exhale, as well as the rise and fall of your chest and the subtle movement of the rest of your body. Observe how your breathing shifts as you focus on it, how it deepens, how it slows down and how it becomes more rhythmic.

In this chapter, we will discuss the power of the breath and the ways in which it can be utilized to bring about a sense of empowered understanding in our daily lives. In this section we will investigate the science behind breathing, various beginner-friendly techniques for mindful breathing and meditation and several ways in which we can incorporate these practices into our day-to-day lives. We will discuss the numerous advantages of practicing mindfulness and breathing exercises, such as lowering levels of stress and anxiety and improving concentration and productivity.

Now that we've taken a moment to compose ourselves, let's take the first step together on this journey. Discovering the power of our breath and all the incredible things it can do for us is a great place to start.

ANATOMY AND PHYSIOLOGY OF THE BREATH—SCIENCE IS COOL

Now, I'm going to tell you what I know you're thinking: "Which comes first, anatomy or physiology? This sounds like the perfect way to get some shut-eye!" If you want to know why meditation is such a powerful tool for calming the mind and body, first and foremost, you need to understand how the breath works. Trust me on this one. And don't just take my word for it—scientific evidence supports it as well.

Let's get down to the fundamentals, shall we? When you take a breath, air enters your trachea via your nose or mouth on its way in. After that, it travels through your bronchial tubes and eventually reaches your lungs. Your lungs are comparable to two spongy balloons, and the air spaces within them are referred to as alveoli. These tiny sacs are where the magic happens: oxygen from the air that you breathe passes through the walls of the alveoli and into your bloodstream. From there, the oxygen can be transported to the cells of your body to keep them alive and well. According to research presented in *Frontiers in Human Neuroscience*, the simple act of deep, focused breathing can increase the amount of oxygen that is delivered to the brain. This, in turn, can lead to improved cognitive function and lower levels of stress.

Now let's talk about what goes on in your body when you take a big breath in and out. You know how when you take a deep breath in and then slowly exhale, you get a sense of calm and relaxation? That is not merely in your head. Your diaphragm moves downward as you take a breath, which causes your chest to expand. Deep, slow breaths allow your lungs to take in more air as they have more space to do so. This causes your body to have a parasympathetic response, which can be thought of as your body's way of saying, "Hey, let's chill out for a minute," when it happens. Your muscles relax, your blood pressure drops and your heart rate slows down. It is the equivalent of pausing the stress response that your body may be experiencing.

This brings us to a vital conclusion: breath is quite literally the cornerstone of a good life. This condensed version of the anatomy and physiology of breathing explains how the physical act of breathing brings oxygen into the body, blood and brain. And if you're still not convinced that the information presented here is fascinating, just think about the fact that the air you're breathing right now has been around for millions of years. Who knows what kind of wild adventures it's been on in its past life? It's possible that it was once living in the lungs of a woolly mammoth or a T-Rex!

THE CONNECTION BETWEEN THE BREATH AND THE NERVOUS SYSTEM

When you are feeling anxious or stressed, you may have heard someone tell you to "take a deep breath." If you managed not to throttle them, you may have realized that deep breath actually helped. Have you ever done this? It now appears that there is some scientific backing for that time-tested recommendation. How you breathe has a direct effect on your nervous system and has the potential to help you experience a sense of calm and relaxation.

So how does it work? Let's first talk about the two branches that make up the nervous system: the sympathetic and the parasympathetic. You can think of the sympathetic nervous system as the alarm system in your body because it gets you ready to either fight or run away in response to a potential threat. The parasympathetic nervous system, on the other hand, functions similarly to a "chill button," assisting you in unwinding and regaining your composure after the danger has passed.

Now, whenever you are confronted with a stressful situation, the sympathetic branch of your nervous system may go into overdrive. Your muscles tense up, your heart rate accelerates and you begin to breathe more quickly and shallowly as a result. However, if you're able to exercise control over your breathing and slow it down, you can stimulate the parasympathetic nervous system, which will allow you to begin experiencing feelings of calm and relaxation. It's almost as if you're using your breathing to activate the "cool down" button! By sending the message to your body that everything is fine by taking slow, deep breaths, you can begin to calm yourself down.

But that's not all: There's also a little thing called the vagus nerve that connects your brain to your internal organs, such as your heart and lungs. This nerve runs from the base of the skull all the way down to the abdomen. You can activate the vagus nerve and further stimulate the parasympathetic nervous system if you slow down the rate at which you breathe. Slow deep breaths relax the body and stimulate the parasympathetic nervous system compared to short breaths that activate a fight-or-flight response. Every time you take a breath, it's as if you're giving your body a warm embrace from the inside.

Therefore, the next time you find yourself feeling stressed or anxious, take a few deep breaths and press that button labeled "chill." If anyone asks why you were breathing like a yoga instructor, simply tell them that you were stimulating your vagus nerve. It's the best possible justification for taking some long, reviving breaths.

BEGINNER BREATH TECHNIQUES

No one would think you need to be taught how to breathe but here you are, reading an introduction to meditation book, so let's talk breathing, fucker.

1. Find a position that allows you to sit comfortably and close your eyes to begin the body scan breathing meditation. Take a long, deep breath in through the nose and then let out your breath completely. Concentrate on the feeling of your breath moving into and out of your body as it enters and exits. Starting at the bottom of your body and slowly working your way up, begin bringing your attention to each body part. Start with your feet and let yourself mentally drift up to your ankle and lower leg, feeling your breath as you go. When you have reached the top of your head, take a deep breath in and then exhale completely. You should feel a sense of relaxation and calm spread throughout your body as a result.

2. Sit in a position that is comfortable for you and close your eyes to begin the counted breath meditation. Take a slow, deep breath in through your nose and count to four as you do. Hold your breath for two counts. Then, slowly exhale out the mouth six counts. Continue this cycle for several minutes while concentrating on the feeling of your breath and the cadence of the count. If you find that your mind is wandering, you can easily bring it back by focusing on your breath and the count. This breath is so awesome to relieve anxiety and get you back to the present fucking moment.

3. Set yourself up in a comfortable seated position and close your eyes to begin the box breathing meditation. Take a slow breath in through your nose for four counts, then hold it for four counts, then slowly exhale for four counts, and finally take another slow breath in for four counts. Continue this cycle for a good number of minutes. Continue concentrating on the feeling of your breath while you count. The practice of box breathing is excellent for reducing feelings of stress and anxiety and helping to calm the mind.

It is essential to keep in mind that meditation is a form of practice, and that it may take some time to achieve mental stillness and maintain concentration on the in and out breaths. Be patient with yourself, and don't give up if at first you find it difficult to concentrate or your mind starts to wander. The more time and effort you put into it, the simpler it will become for you to still your mind and maintain your concentration on the breath.

Let's get a little more advanced, because it's just fuckin' breathing. These are easy, too, so don't sweat it. Relax and let's do this.

1. Alternate nostril breathing: While engaging in deep breathing, practice this technique by alternating between closing and opening each nostril. Find a comfortable sitting position, close your eyes, then place the thumb of your right hand over your right nostril. After taking a long, slow breath in through your left nostril, gently press your ring finger against your left nostril to close it, and then release your right nostril. Breathe out through your right nostril, followed by a breath in through your right nostril, and finally, breathe out through your left nostril. It is believed that this technique promotes relaxation as well as a balance between the left and right hemispheres of the brain.

2. Ujjayi breath: Creating a sound that is gentle and reminiscent of the ocean, this technique involves controlling the breath while also partially closing the glottis, which is the space between the vocal cords. Find a comfortable sitting position, close your eyes and take deep breaths, concentrating on the sound of your breath as it enters and exits your body. With your mouth closed, inhale through your nose, and on the exhale constrict your throat like you're fogging a mirror. This breath can make you sound like Darth Vader, too, so that is fun if you dabble in the dark side. During meditation, this method can help bring calmness to the mind and increase focus.

3. Kapalabhati breathing: In this technique, exhalations are made with more force than usual, followed by inhalations made more slowly. Find a comfortable sitting position, close your eyes and concentrate on your breath. Take a long, slow breath in, and then let out your breath as quickly and forcefully as you can, tensing your abdominal muscles as you do so. Continue this pattern for a few minutes while concentrating on the feeling of the breath as it enters and exits your body. It is believed that practicing kapalabhati breathing can help release tension that has built up in the body as well as stimulate the body's energy.

STAYIN' ALIVE: BREATHING THROUGH THE BUSY

Even though breathing is a fundamental component of our everyday lives, it can be challenging to bring conscious awareness to this process at times. Fortunately, there are a few straightforward methods that you can use to incorporate breathing practices into your daily routine without the activity becoming a burden. The following are some suggestions that should make it easier for you to breathe:

Take a Breath Break

Take a moment to relax and breathe instead of stopping for a cup of coffee. Remind yourself to take some slow, deep breaths about once every hour or so by setting a timer on your phone or computer. Your coworkers might give you strange looks, but who cares? You are the one who will experience feelings of renewal and revitalization!

Use Breathing as an Excuse

Do you need an alibi to get out of attending that tedious meeting or ending that drawn-out phone call? Simply say that you are trying to clear your mind by taking some long, slow breaths. You won't have to worry about anyone disagreeing with you, and you'll have some time to yourself to de-stress.

Make It a Game

Create a game out of your breathing exercises by setting a timer for 1 minute and seeing how many deep breaths you can take in that amount of time. If you can pull it off without feeling lightheaded, you earn an extra point.

Sing It Out

Take a few slow, deep breaths, and then sing out loud your favorite song. It will feel awkward at first, but doing so is a fantastic way to increase the amount of oxygen that is circulating through your body, not to mention that it is a lot of fun!

The act of breathing is a miraculous and intricate process that we frequently disregard as unimportant. Most of us ignore the significance of our breath, which acts as a continual reminder that we are alive (and part of the living, breathing world around us). But, if you cultivate the habit of paying attention to your breath, you can use it as a source of strength as well as serenity and clarity. This can have a parasympathetic response on your body, allowing you to relax and reducing the levels of stress and anxiety you experience, which allows you to deepen your breath, slow it down and make it more rhythmic.

Overall, the power of breath is immense, and if you incorporate mindfulness and breathing exercises into your daily routines, you can experience a wide range of positive effects. These include a reduction in the symptoms of anxiety and depression, improved concentration, bolstered productivity and the promotion of a sense of calm and relaxation. The breath is a constant companion that you can use to improve both your general health and the quality of your life. You will be able to realize the full potential of this process that maintains life if you're willing to invest the time and effort required to investigate the many methods and approaches.

MIND

BODY

CHAPTER 6

GET IN TOUCH WITH YO' SELF— EXPLORING THE BODY

MIND-BODY CONNECTION

"What exactly does it mean when people talk about the mind–body connection, and why should I care?" Let me tell you something very important: The connection between your mind and body is like Batman and Robin for your health. Although at first glance they appear to be two distinct entities, when working together they form a powerful force that is capable of kicking some serious butt. BAM!

Let's get the fundamentals out of the way first. The concept that your thoughts, feelings and beliefs can affect your physical health is referred to as the mind–body connection. In other words, your body may experience physical symptoms such as headaches, fatigue and muscle tension if you are stressed out, anxious or depressed. On the other hand, your body may respond with feelings of well-being and good health if you are happy, relaxed and content.

Now, I am aware you might be thinking that this sounds like some new age woo-woo nonsense. However, you don't have to take my word for it because it's supported by scientific studies. Mindfulness meditation has been shown to reduce inflammation in the body, which is linked to a variety of health problems such as heart disease, diabetes and cancer, according to Carnegie Mellon University.

But hold on, there's more to it! Your mental state and the feelings you experience can even change your DNA. Yes, folks, you read that correctly: You can literally think yourself healthy. Participants in a study (published in the journal *Frontiers in Immunology*) that engaged in mindfulness-based stress reduction saw changes in the expression of genes that are involved in inflammation and immune function. According to the findings of the study, mindfulness meditation may be responsible for the positive changes in gene expression that are associated with improved health outcomes.

Now you can see the connection between the mind and the body is not just some new-age concept; rather, there is actual science that supports this link. If you give your mind the attention it needs, your body will respond favorably. Also, when you take care of your body, you will find that it brings happiness to your mind as well. The outcome is beneficial for both entities.

THE STRESS RESPONSE: WHEN YOUR BODY THINKS IT'S A CAVEMAN

Oh, the wonderful feeling of panic and dread that can overtake you at the most inopportune times—it's called stress. But were you aware that the stress response your body produces is an ancient survival mechanism that dates to our ancestors who lived in caves? When our ancestors from prehistoric times were threatened, their bodies went into a state known as "fight or flight," in which their systems were flooded with hormones designed to help them either fight the danger in front of them or flee it. This gave them the ability to choose between the two options.

Even though we do not have to worry about saber-toothed tigers or woolly mammoths, our bodies react in the same way to stress, and this has not changed in a few thousand years. When we are under stress, our brains produce hormones like cortisol and adrenaline that get our bodies ready for action. This can be caused by a looming deadline at work, a fight with a loved one or even just the everyday stresses of modern life.

What takes place inside of us when we allow ourselves to become stressed? First, our heart rate and blood pressure both go up, which over time can put strain on our cardiovascular system. In addition, our immune systems may become compromised, and we may suffer from muscle tension, headaches and digestive problems. In fact, a study that was published in the *Malaysian Journal of Medical Sciences* found that chronic stress can suppress the immune system, making us more prone to getting sick.

However, the effects of stress are not limited to the body. When we are under constant pressure, it can also have a negative impact on our mental health. Anxiety, depression, insomnia and even memory problems have been linked to chronic stress, along with decreased productivity and poor decision-making skills, as well as other negative outcomes.

The question is, what can you do to fight the harmful effects of stress? Although you may not be able to completely remove stress from your life, you can become better at managing it if you make the effort. Meditation, yoga or even something as simple as taking a few slow, deep breaths are all examples of practices that can help you calm down. The practice of mindfulness meditation has been shown to help reduce symptoms of anxiety and depression, as well as lower blood pressure and improve the quality of sleep, according to the National Center for Complementary and Integrative Health.

Also, let's not forget the significance of practicing self-care, which can consist of anything from indulging in a guilty pleasure like watching trashy reality TV to taking a soothing bath or going for a walk in the great outdoors. Developing resilience and improving our ability to deal with the pressures of everyday life can be facilitated by prioritizing self-care and paying attention to the present moment.

HOW MEDITATION CAN HELP YOU CHILL OUT AND STOP STRESSING (LIKE, FOR REAL)

So far, we've discussed how stress can seriously wreak havoc on your body and leave you feeling like a complete and utter train wreck. However, you shouldn't be concerned, my friend. There is a way out of this predicament, and it does not involve taking any more Xanax. (However, if you already have a prescription for it, you should follow that instead. No judgment here.)

The answer, in case you were wondering ... is ... (drum roll, please) MEDITATION! Indeed, you have it correct. And there is, in fact, some credible scientific research that supports the claims that your eccentric, meditating aunt has been making for years about this particular topic. Who would have guessed?

Let's analyze it in more detail. As we discussed in the previous section, when you're under a lot of pressure, your body prepares itself to either fight or run away, as if your inner caveman is getting ready to either flee from or battle a saber-toothed tiger to the death. (You probably don't have to worry about this scenario—unless, of course, you're employed at a zoo. Then you should probably watch your back.)

But, although most of us aren't really in any kind of life-threatening peril, we are stressed out about everything that life throws at us, whether it's work, school, relationships or anything else. Our bodies are therefore stuck in this state of high alert, with our heart rates increasing and our muscles becoming tense. It is as if our bodies are constantly revving their engines, but they are never actually allowed to go anywhere.

MOVEMENT

MEDITATION

Meditation is a practice that can help with this. By practicing meditation, you stimulate your parasympathetic nervous system, which has the effect of slowing down your body's natural response to stress.

So, in what ways can you actually benefit? As already mentioned, meditation has been shown to reduce symptoms of anxiety and depression, as well as lower levels of the stress hormone cortisol, according to a study published in *Psychology Research and Behavior Management*.

In a nutshell, the act of meditating is analogous to providing your body with a much-needed vacation from the effects of stress . . . the equivalent of giving your body some much-needed R&R at a luxurious beach resort in the Caribbean (or wherever your idea of paradise may be). Who doesn't feel like they could use more of that in their life?

Therefore, the next time you feel like you're about to lose your cool, take a few moments to breathe deeply and give meditation a shot. It is possible that you will be surprised by how much of a difference it can make.

MOVEMENT MEDITATION—BECAUSE THAT BOOTY NEEDS TO MOVE

Okay, everyone, pay attention here! In just a moment, we are going to embark on an adventure into the wondrous world of movement meditation. And before you ask, we are not referring to the type of movement that occurs after consuming a burrito that is particularly spicy. This is an entirely unique style of movement.

You might be wondering what exactly "movement meditation" entails, and it is exactly what it sounds like: making use of movement as a method of meditation. So, let's move your fuckin' body.

On a more serious note, there are many ways to practice movement meditation. It can be as uncomplicated as going for a walk in the woods and focusing on being present in the moment, or it can be as regimented as participating in a tai chi or hot yoga class. The most important thing is that every movement you make with your body is done consciously and with intention.

You might be asking yourself at this point, "Why on earth would I want to do movement meditation when I can just sit on my couch and watch an entire season of a show on Netflix in one sitting?" The answer to that question is easy: Because, well, duh, it's healthy for you!

The practice of movement meditation has been shown to have a variety of positive effects on both the mind and the body. For instance, one study in the journal *Psychiatric Clinics of North America* found that tai chi can help reduce symptoms of depression and anxiety. And let's be honest: who doesn't want a little less stress and anxiety?

The practice of movement meditation has also been shown to improve one's physical health. Yoga has been shown to lower blood pressure and reduce the risk of developing heart disease, as stated in the journal *Evidence-Based Complementary and Alternative Medicine*. This is a win–win situation, especially considering that you get to wear those adorable yoga pants.

Therefore, if you are prepared to advance to the next level of your meditation practice, you should try incorporating some movement into your routine. Simply getting moving and being present in the moment can be accomplished through a variety of activities, including dancing to your favorite song or performing some gentle stretches. And if anyone asks you why you are twirling around like a ballerina in the park, just tell them that you are engaging in some movement meditation. Even if they give you a strange look, you won't care because you'll be the one who's feeling fabulous and Zen.

TYPES OF MEDITATION FOR THE BODY

Body Scan Meditation

Have you reached a point where you are sick of blowing all of your hard-earned money on extravagant trips to far-off lands? You don't even have to leave the house (or office, or car or wherever you happen to be) to experience the serenity of a vacation thanks to a practice called body scan meditation. All you require is a relaxing spot to lie down and the ability to concentrate on the myriad aches and pains present throughout your body.

To begin, find a place to lie down that is comfortable for you, close your eyes then take a long, deep breath in through your nose and out through your mouth. Now, concentrate on each and every part of your body, beginning at the top of your head and working your way down.

Take a moment to focus on your head and become aware of any feelings of tension or discomfort that you might be experiencing. You could be suffering from a headache, or it could be that your jaw is clenched. Acknowledge whatever it is, then let it go. Visualize that headache being swept away. Unclench your jaw. Moving on to your face, note any creases or furrows that may be present, and visualize them being smoothed out like a shirt that has just been ironed.

Next focus on your neck and shoulders. Because this is where many of us store a lot of tension, really concentrate your attention on these areas for a moment. Imagine any knots or tightness in your muscles vanishing like ice cream on a hot summer day as you stretch them out.

As you continue your scan down to your arms, hands and fingers, stop for a moment and pay attention to whether you are experiencing any tingling or numbness. Imagine that any tension you're feeling is being released through your fingertips like water from a tap.

Moving on to the front and back of your chest, feel the expansion and contraction of your ribcage as you take a long, deep breath in then out. Imagine having a team of experienced massage therapists work their magic on your back to relieve any aches, pains or tension that might be there.

Take a moment to focus on any discomfort or bloating you may be experiencing as you move down to your stomach and hips. Imagine all of your aches and pains melting away as a warm blanket wraps you in its embrace. And at long last, you've arrived at your lower extremities, the legs and feet. If you have any aches or pains, imagine that a group of tiny, magical gnomes are massaging them away (because who doesn't enjoy a good gnome massage?).

You won't have to leave the house or spend any money to experience the benefits of this full-body meditation that will leave you feeling relaxed and revitalized. So, the next time you find yourself feeling stressed or overwhelmed, just keep this in mind: You can always treat yourself to a mini-vacation by meditating on your body.

The Sensory Overload

Are you finding that the nonstop onslaught of sights, sounds and smells that make up the world around us are overstimulating? Prepare yourself for the sensory overload that is meditation, in which you will learn to tune out the outside world and concentrate on your inner self (or the voice in your head, whichever you prefer). You only need a calm place to sit and the ability to concentrate on what your senses are telling you.

To begin, find a nice spot to sit, close your eyes and make a conscious effort to inhale deeply through your nose and exhale through your mouth. Now, to get started, begin to tune out the outside world and concentrate on the world within yourself. First, put your attention on how well you can hear. Take a moment to focus your attention on the sounds in your immediate environment, then try to

picture turning down the volume as if you were operating a radio. Soon enough, the sounds begin to dissipate one by one until you are left with nothing but the sound of silence.

Your next step tunes in to your sight. Take a moment to focus on a specific light or color, then picture yourself turning down the intensity of that light or color as you would a dimmer switch. The light gradually decreases until all you can see is darkness.

Moving on to your sense of smell, take a moment to become aware of any odors in your immediate environment, then visualize dialing back the potency of those odors. The aromas should become less noticeable until all that is left to smell is void.

Last but not least, pay attention to your sense of touch. Take a moment to become aware of any sensations that are occurring on your skin, then picture yourself lowering the temperature or intensity of those sensations using a thermostat. The sensation eventually disappears, and all that is left is a void in your body.

You won't have to go anywhere or spend any money to enjoy this sensory overload meditation that will leave you feeling relaxed and revitalized. Remember that you can always tune out the outside world by practicing some good old-fashioned sensory overload meditation the next time you find yourself feeling overwhelmed or overstimulated.

The Body as a Friend

Do you often find yourself alone and yearning for the company of others? Through practicing the meditation titled "Body as a Friend," you will be able to transform your physical self into your new best friend. The time has come to cultivate a friendly relationship with your own body BFF. You only need a place to sit that is comfortable and the ability to concentrate on your body to do this exercise.

Sitting comfortably, close your eyes, then take a long, deep breath in through your nose and out through your mouth. First, let's spend some time getting acquainted with your new best friend—your body.

Bring your attention to your head. Take a moment to become aware of any feelings of tension or discomfort that you might be experiencing. Imagine that your head is a wise old sage who is constantly offering you words of advice and direction.

The next area to concentrate on is your neck and shoulders. Take a moment to become aware of any aches or pains that you might be experiencing. Imagine that the strong and reliable support system that is always there to hold you up is your neck and shoulders.

As you move on to your arms and hands, take a moment to become aware of any sensations that you might be experiencing. Imagine that your arms and hands are the ones offering assistance to those who are in need, and that you are always prepared to do so.

Slowly move your attention to your ribcage and chest, then take a deep breath in and out while feeling your ribcage expand and contract with each inhale and exhale. Imagine that the core of the issue is located in your chest and back, and that it is always there to keep you going.

Take a moment to focus on any sensation you may be feeling in your stomach and hips as you move down to that region of your body. Imagine that your stomach and hips are the center of your being and that they always keep you anchored.

Last but not least, pay attention to your legs and feet. Take note of any sensations that you might be experiencing. Imagine the foundation of your being is your legs and feet, and that they always ensure you remain steady and strong.

A meditation on the body as a friend will leave you feeling relaxed and refreshed, all without having to go anywhere or spend any money. The next time you find yourself experiencing feelings of isolation, just keep in mind that you now have a new best friend right there with you: your own body.

Yoga and Meditation, a Match Made in Heaven

Have you reached a point in your meditation practice where you are bored with just sitting still? It's time to get moving! By incorporating yoga into your meditation practice, you can add some much-needed movement into the mix, making it a more complete practice. All that is required is a relaxing environment in which to move as well as some degree of flexibility (but don't worry, we'll help you improve that as well).

To begin, find a place that is comfortable for you to practice, and roll out your yoga mat there. We'll start with some basic yoga postures.

Now, find a seated position that is both comfortable and stable, such as easy pose (sukhasana) or lotus pose (padmasana). Put your hands over your eyes and take a few deep breaths, in through your nose and out through your mouth. Close your eyes. Now, incorporate some movement into the routine by adopting the posture known as the cat–cow (marjaryasana–bitilasana). You should create a gentle arch in your back by lowering your belly toward the mat as you inhale and then lifting your head and tailbone toward the sky as you exhale. As you let your breath out, curl your spine upward toward the ceiling and tuck your chin in toward your chest. Perform this movement several times, making sure to synchronize your breathing with each repetition.

Following that, incorporate some standing postures. To begin, get into mountain pose (tadasana) by standing with your feet hip-distance apart and your arms by your sides. Take a few slow, deep breaths and raise both arms above your head while reaching upward toward the heavens. In the forward bend (uttanasana), as you exhale, bend forward from your hips and reach toward your toes. Perform this movement several times, making sure to synchronize your breathing with each repetition.

As we get closer to the end of our practice, incorporate some restorative postures. Begin by moving into corpse pose (savasana) by lying flat on your back. Bring both of your knees up to your chest, and then wrap your arms around them to get into a comfortable position. Take a long, slow breath in and out, then give yourself permission to relax completely into the posture.

A combination of yoga and meditation can be a great equalizer, giving you energy yet relaxing you at the same time. The next time you feel as though your meditation practice is becoming a little monotonous, just keep in mind that you can always incorporate some yoga into the mix. Best wishes as you stretch!

HEALING AND RELAXATION: USING MEDITATION TO PROMOTE PHYSICAL WELL-BEING

Are you ready to find physical well-being through healing and relaxation? In the next sections, let's explore how to relax and heal your body and mind. You know you want to.

Pain Relief Meditation

Feeling like you've been run over by a truck? Let's find some relief with the power of meditation. Through the practice of meditation, you can turn down the volume on that pain and make it more bearable. For pain management and relief, I recommend mindfulness meditation. To practice mindfulness meditation, all you require is a quiet, comfortable place to sit and the ability to concentrate on your breath.

Locate a place to sit that is comfortable. Remember you can do this seated, on a meditation cushion, chair or lying down. Close your eyes, then take a long, deep breath in through your nose and out through your mouth. Concentrate on your breath. Take note of any pain or discomfort. First, you must acknowledge the pain or discomfort in order to let go of it. Take a few slow, deep breaths, and as you let them out, picture the discomfort leaving your body like air being let out of a balloon.

Put your attention on your breath, and let your mind drift. Imagine that your breath is moving like a gentle wave, flowing in and out of your body as you breathe in and out. Imagine this gentle wave washing over you, reducing the pain as each wave rolls through.

As you bring your attention to your breathing, pay attention to any thoughts or feelings that may come up. Recognize and accept them before letting go of your attachment to them by allowing them to just be without any judgment or labels. Just notice them come and go without any control, and redirect your attention to your breathing.

This straightforward meditation technique, despite its apparent simplicity, can be quite helpful in alleviating pain and other unpleasant sensations. Therefore, the next time you experience pain, just keep in mind that you have the ability to reduce the intensity of that pain through the practice of meditation.

Even though research has shown that meditation can be helpful for pain management, it is imperative that patients seek the advice of a qualified medical professional prior to beginning any new pain management routine. Additionally, patients should not use meditation as a replacement for conventional medical treatment.

Walking Meditation

As a form of mindfulness meditation, walking meditation is a technique that is gaining more and more popularity according to PositivePsychology.com. Walking meditation is a mindfulness practice that entails paying attention to the here and now and being completely conscious of your surroundings as you go about your daily routine. This type of meditation can be practiced pretty much anywhere, so long as there is enough room to move around.

Choose a location that is free from distractions and is easy for strolling. This may be a placid park, a winding path or even in a room in your house. Examine your surroundings carefully to ensure that you have sufficient room to move around freely and that there are no obstructions in your path.

After selecting an appropriate place, take a few moments to center yourself by standing at the far end of the space. Take a few calm, deep breaths, exhale them as slowly as you can, then let your body relax. Start off walking slowly but steadily, paying attention to the sensation of your feet making contact with the earth with each step.

Maintain awareness of both your breath and the sensations occurring throughout your body as you walk, perhaps becoming aware of the sensation of the sun on your skin or the wind in your hair. Make an effort to be in the here and now and let go of any thoughts or distractions that may come to mind.

During walking meditation, it is standard practice to repeat a phrase or mantra to oneself as a way to maintain focus. You may say to yourself something along the lines of "I am present in this moment" or "I am grounded and at ease." When you repeat the phrase, try to let go of any negative ideas or feelings and instead focus your attention on the positive energy you are creating.

Walk for an allotted amount of time, which could be anything from 10 to 15 minutes. When your allotted time has expired, come to a stop as gradually as possible and then take a few long, deep breaths. Take some time to think about what you went through and how it made you feel. During a session of walking meditation, you could discover that you feel both more relaxed and more concentrated than before.

In a nutshell, the practice of walking meditation is moving through your environment while maintaining an awareness of yourself and the world around you. It is an excellent method for cultivating awareness, and it can be done in any location. You can let go of distractions and bad ideas and feel calmer and more at peace if you focus on your breath, the sensations in your body and a mantra or phrase.

CHAPTER 7

THOUGHTS AND FEELINGS? FUCK 'EM AND FEEL 'EM

THOUGHTS VERSUS FEELINGS: WHAT'S THE DIFFERENCE?

Have you ever had trouble determining whether you were just thinking about something or whether you were actually feeling it? Understanding the distinction between your thoughts and feelings is essential for anyone who wants to improve their mental and emotional health through the practice of meditation, despite the fact that the distinction can be a bit of a head scratcher at times.

So, let's analyze it step by step. The ideas and mental pictures that come to your mind, most frequently in response to some sort of stimulus, are referred to as thoughts. They can be conscious or unconscious, and they can range from being straightforward and everyday, to being convoluted and esoteric. Thoughts such as "I need to pick up milk at the store" or "What if I don't get that promotion?" are both examples.

On the other hand, feelings are the bodily sensations that occur on the inside of a person in response to either their thoughts or the happenings in the outside world. They are often accompanied by a label or name that helps you identify the emotion that you are experiencing, and they can be described as bodily sensations such as warmth, heaviness, tension and tingling. The expressions "I feel happy when I spend time with my friends" and "I feel anxious when I have to speak in public" are both examples of feelings.

Although our thoughts and feelings are frequently intertwined and can mutually affect one another, it is essential to be able to differentiate between the two, because thoughts are more susceptible to change than feelings, which are frequently more powerful and persistent than thoughts. In fact, studies have shown that it can be challenging to try to change our feelings directly, but that changing our thoughts can have a significant impact on our emotional experiences.

Take a moment, stop what you're doing and tune in to how your body is responding the next time you're trying to determine whether something is going through your head or your heart. Pay attention to the sensations that are occurring in your body and try to determine which word or phrase most accurately encapsulates the feeling you are currently experiencing. Also, keep in mind that although your thoughts and feelings are important, they are also fleeting and can change at any time. We can cultivate a greater sense of mental and emotional equilibrium by learning, through the practice of meditation, to observe and comprehend our own thoughts and feelings without allowing ourselves to become overpowered by them.

THOUGHTS IN MEDITATION

You might be sitting comfortably with your eyes closed, taking several long, deep breaths and making an effort to concentrate on your breathing as you begin your meditation practice. Nonetheless, you rapidly become aware that a thought is distracting you from the task at hand. In spite of your best efforts to put it out of your mind, it keeps creeping back into your consciousness, and before you know it, you are inundated with a flood of ideas, submerged in a sea of thoughts, which can feel very overpowering.

Keep in mind that having such an experience during meditation is not at all unusual. In fact, nearly everyone who engages in the practice of meditation encounters thoughts that take on a variety of shapes and forms. The following is a list of some of the most typical categories of thoughts that may come to mind while meditating:

- Worrying: Thoughts that revolve around fears, concerns or uncertainties about the future or past.

- Planning: Thoughts about what needs to be done, how to do it and when to do it.

- Fantasizing: Thoughts that involve daydreaming, imagining or reminiscing about something pleasurable or exciting.

- Judging: Thoughts that involve evaluating oneself or others, criticizing or comparing.

- Analyzing: Thoughts that involve trying to understand or solve a problem, puzzle or issue.

- Remembering: Thoughts that involve recalling a memory, experience or person.

Having these thoughts while meditating is a natural and expected part of the practice and should not be a cause for alarm. Acknowledge them and allow them to recede without passing judgment on them, rather than trying to drive them away. You can develop a greater sense of mindfulness and inner peace by just acknowledging and watching your thoughts.

NAVIGATING FEELINGS IN MEDITATION

You're attempting to meditate, sitting with your legs crossed, eyes closed and taking some deep breaths. But hold on, what feeling is that? Oh, fuck me, here we go.

Feelings are an inevitable component of the human experience, and they can be particularly distracting when one is attempting to practice meditation. But do not be afraid, because I am here to walk you through the mental roller coaster that is meditation and feelings.

It's important to get this out of the way right off the bat, so here it is: There is no such thing as positive or negative feelings. Every emotion is real, and having them is an inevitable and natural part of being a human being. Therefore, if you are meditating and you start to feel something, don't try to push it away or judge it. Instead, simply acknowledge the feeling. Simply admit that it is happening, then let it go.

Now, let's talk about some of the more common feelings that may arise during your meditation practice. It's wonderful if you're able to find some inner serenity and calm. On the other hand, you might experience feelings of agitation, anxiety or even boredom—and that's perfectly fine as well. Remember that there are no positive or negative feelings; they just are.

During meditation, using your breath as an anchor is one of the most effective ways to navigate your feelings and thoughts. When you notice that your mind is beginning to wander, bring your attention back to your breathing. Inhale deeply, pause for a few seconds, then slowly exhale all that air out of your lungs. Do this as many times as is required.

One more useful strategy is to name the emotions you're experiencing. When you become aware of a new sensation, label it as soon as you can. Tell yourself something like, "I'm feeling anxious right now," for example, if you're experiencing symptoms of anxiety. By giving a name to the sensation, you are able to put some distance between yourself and the emotion, which makes it easier for you to observe it without becoming engulfed.

And, keep in mind that feelings are fleeting; they can change quickly. They move through the air much like clouds in the sky. Therefore, don't become overly attached to any particular feeling. Simply take note of it, admit that you're aware of it, then let it go.

Having feelings during the meditation process is both a normal and natural occurrence. Just observe them without passing judgment. Make use of the breath as an anchor, name the feelings you're experiencing and keep in mind that they are only temporary.

DEALING WITH PANIC AND ANXIETY DURING MEDITATION— LIONS AND TIGERS AND STEPPING ON LEGOS, OH MY!

Finding your inner peace is the primary goal of meditation; however, what happens when your inner peace is shattered by emotions such as panic and anxiety? You might begin to feel as though you are suffocating in a room full of people, or you might begin to sweat like you are in a hot yoga class. Both scenarios are possible, but friends, there is no need to be afraid; we are going to talk about how to deal with panic and anxiety during meditation, all while maintaining a sense of humor about the situation.

To begin, let's talk about panic attacks. They have the potential to be terrifying, but they do not pose a threat to your life. They are your body's way of letting you know that you need to take some deep breaths and relax. You might have the sensation that you're having a heart attack or that you're about to pass away, but you won't. Unless, of course, you're reading this while skydiving without a parachute. If that is the case, I will be unable to assist you. For everyone else, however, take a few slow, deep breaths and keep in mind that panic attacks are temporary.

Now, anxiety: It can be a tricky little devil, sneaking up on you when you least expect it. Anxiety can make you worry about things that you wouldn't normally worry about, like whether your cat is hatching a plan to murder you while you snooze. Believe me when I say that your cat is probably too preoccupied with dozing off to plot anything. However, being completely serious, anxiety can be a real pain in the ass.

The question is, what can you do if feelings of anxiety or panic start to emerge during your meditation practice? The following are some important considerations:

1. Acknowledge the feeling. Don't try to push it away or ignore it. Just accept that it's there, and let it pass. Think of it like an annoying relative who always shows up uninvited. Just smile, say hello, then usher them out the door.

2. Focus on your breath. Take deep, slow breaths and imagine that you're inhaling calm and exhaling stress. Imagine that with each breath, you're blowing away your worries like a dandelion. Breathe in through your nose and count to four, hold your breath for two counts, then exhale out your mouth for six counts.

3. Try visualization. Picture yourself in a place that makes you feel calm and happy. It could be a beach, a forest or a cozy armchair by a fireplace. Visualize every detail, from the sounds to the smells to the textures.

4. Give yourself a break. If you're feeling too overwhelmed, take a break from meditation. There's no shame in admitting that you're not in the right headspace for it. Go for a walk, do some yoga or watch some funny cat videos on YouTube. It's not a failure to acknowledge what you need in the moment.

If you want to improve your mental and emotional health through meditation, you must learn to differentiate between your ideas and feelings. Feelings are internal physiological sensations that occur in response to your thoughts or the events of the outside world, while thoughts are the mental images that enter your mind. While thoughts are more susceptible to change, feelings are typically more powerful and persistent. In meditation, it is not rare to meet different types of thoughts, including worrying, planning, dreaming, judging, analyzing and remembering. Similarly, emotions are a natural aspect of being human, yet they can easily disrupt your meditation practice. However, by simply recognizing cognitive and emotional experiences without judgment, you can cultivate deeper awareness and inner serenity. By learning to examine and grasp thoughts and feelings, you can create a greater sense of mental and emotional stability.

POSITIVITY

CHAPTER 8

AFFIRMATIONS AND MANTRAS—THE FUCKIN' POWER OF POSITIVE THINKING

YOU'VE PROBABLY HEARD THE SAYING "FAKE IT UNTIL YOU MAKE IT." So, when it comes to mantras and affirmations, that is precisely what we are going to do, I promise you that. Because, let's be real, if you're going to be stuck with the same thoughts in your head all day, you might as well make them positive ones rather than negative.

Both affirmations and mantras are similar in that they involve the repetition of positive statements or words as a means of promoting personal growth and change. But, there are a number of significant distinctions between the two.

Affirmations are statements that an individual makes to themselves that are positive and empowering to assist them in overcoming negative thoughts, beliefs or habits. Affirmations frequently concentrate on either the present or the future, and their primary functions are to boost one's sense of self-confidence and self-esteem as well as one's motivation. For instance, an affirmation could be something along the lines of "I am deserving of love and respect" or "I am capable of achieving my goals."

Mantras are brief phrases that are repeated as a tool for concentration and meditation. They can help you achieve a state of inner peace and clarity, and are frequently utilized in Eastern spiritual traditions like Buddhism and Hinduism. Mantras can be thought of as a form of mental meditation. Mantras are typically uttered in Sanskrit or one of a number of other languages. They can be recited silently or out loud. One example of a mantra that is frequently utilized in Buddhist and Hindu meditation practices is the word "om."

So, to recap: Affirmations are self-statements that are used to boost confidence and self-esteem, and mantras are repetitive phrases that are used in meditation and other forms of spiritual practice.

THE IMPORTANCE OF CONSISTENT USE OF AFFIRMATIONS

Affirmations, much like plants, require consistent care and attention if you want them to bear fruit in the form of growth. Unfortunately, unlike a Crock-Pot™ you can turn on and walk away from, maintaining a consistent practice with your affirmations is necessary if you wish to derive the maximum benefit.

Imagine that your affirmations are like a membership to a gym. You can't just expect to see results after signing up for a gym membership and going there once. That won't cut it. You need to work hard and maintain a consistent presence to see results. Affirmations are the same in this regard. You can't just repeat them once and expect your life to suddenly become different in a miraculous way.

Affirmations, when used on a regular basis, can assist in the formation of new neural pathways in the brain. It's very similar to cutting a new trail through an overgrown jungle. The more you travel along that path, the more you will notice how clear and simple the way ahead has become. In the end, it turns out to be the route with the least amount of difficulty.

However, using affirmations consistently can be challenging, much like maintaining a gym membership. It is simple to forget, to become preoccupied or to be just plain unmotivated. So, it's critical to incorporate the use of positive affirmations into a consistent routine. Find a time of day that is conducive, whether it be first thing in the morning or right before you go to sleep. Make affirmations a mandatory part of your daily routine, just like brushing your teeth or taking a shower, and you won't have any choice but to practice.

Consistency is key when it comes to affirmations. If you want to see results, you need to make sure you use them on a consistent basis. Therefore, put in the effort, be present and watch how your life will change. Don't worry if you happen to go a few days without making use of them. It's not the end of the world, any more than skipping a workout at the gym is going to ruin your life. Simply get back on track as soon as you are able to and continue forward.

PRACTICING AFFIRMATIONS

Practicing affirmations involves repeating positive statements to yourself on a regular basis. Here are some steps to help you get started with affirmations:

1. Choose affirmations that resonate with you: Select affirmations that align with your goals and values. You can find affirmations related to self-esteem, self-confidence and other areas you want to work on.

2. Repeat affirmations regularly: Repetition is key to making affirmations effective. Say them in the morning, throughout the day or before going to bed. The more often you repeat affirmations, the more likely you are to internalize the positive beliefs and attitudes they convey.

3. Speak affirmations with conviction: Say the affirmations as if they are already true, and feel the positive emotions associated with the affirmation.

4. Write affirmations down to reinforce the positive beliefs and attitudes they convey: You can write affirmations in a journal, on sticky notes or on the notes app of your phone.

5. Practice visualization: Along with repeating affirmations, imagine yourself living out the positive beliefs and attitudes expressed in the affirmations. This can help to increase the effectiveness of affirmations and promote a greater sense of well-being.

Here are ten powerful personal affirmations that you can use to help build a positive mindset and achieve your goals:

1. I am capable of achieving anything I set my mind to.

2. I am deserving of love, respect and happiness.

3. I trust my intuition and make decisions that align with my values and goals.

4. I am continuously growing and evolving as a person.

5. I am confident in myself and my abilities.

6. I am responsible for my own happiness and success.

7. I am grateful for all the positive experiences and people in my life.

8. I release all negative thoughts and emotions and focus on the present moment.

9. I am open to new opportunities and experiences that will help me grow.

10. I am a valuable and unique individual, worthy of love and respect.

Affirmations should be used with patience and persistence because they need time and repetition to work. Making affirmations a regular part of your daily routine can help ensure that you utilize them frequently, which is essential if you want to reap their full benefits. By doing this, you can improve your outlook on life, encourage growth and accomplish your objectives.

PRACTICING MANTRA MEDITATION

Practicing mantra-based meditation is relatively simple and can be done by following these steps:

1. Choose a mantra that resonates with you, or use a traditional mantra such as "om" or "so hum."

2. Find a quiet place and comfortable place to sit where you won't be disturbed. You can sit in a chair or on the floor, whichever is more comfortable for you.

3. Set your intention for your meditation practice. Focus on why you are doing this meditation and what you hope to gain.

4. Focus on your breath: Take a few deep breaths and focus on the sensation of your breath as it moves in and out of your body.

5. Repeat the mantra: Once you have established a peaceful and relaxed state, start repeating the mantra silently in your mind and continue as many times as you like.

6. Stay focused: It's normal for your mind to wander during meditation so if this happens, simply notice the thought and bring your focus back to your mantra.

7. End the meditation: After a few minutes, slowly open your eyes and take a deep breath. Take a moment to notice how you feel and what has changed since you began your meditation.

8. Practice regularly: Mantra-based meditation is most effective when practiced regularly, so aim to make it a part of your daily routine.

Here are 10 powerful mantras you can use for meditation or daily affirmations:

1. Om: This is a traditional mantra and is considered the most sacred sound in Hinduism. It is believed to represent the sound of the universe.

2. Gayatri mantra: This mantra is believed to bring wisdom, enlightenment and spiritual growth. It is one of the most powerful mantras in Hinduism.

3. Om namah Shivaya: This mantra is associated with Lord Shiva and is believed to help in purifying the mind and body. It is a popular mantra for those seeking spiritual growth and transformation.

4. Lokah samastah sukhino bhavantu: This Sanskrit mantra translates to "May all beings everywhere be happy and free, and may the thoughts, words and actions of my own life contribute in some way to that happiness and to that freedom for all."

5. Om shanti: This is a peaceful mantra that is often used to help calm the mind and reduce stress and anxiety.

6. So hum: This is a simple but powerful mantra that means "I am that." It is used to help connect with the divine consciousness that resides within us all.

7. Om mani padme hum: This is a Buddhist mantra that is believed to usher in compassion, peace and enlightenment.

8. Ra ma da sa: This is a Kundalini mantra that is believed to bring healing energy to the body and mind.

9. Sat nam: This is another Kundalini mantra that means "truth is my identity." It is used to help connect with the inner self and bring clarity and focus.

10. Hare Krishna: This is a mantra often associated with the Hare Krishna movement and is believed to bring devotion, love and happiness.

It is easy and effective to create inner calm and relieve tension using mantra-based meditation. You can establish a daily meditation practice that can help you manage anxiety and enhance your general well-being by following these steps: selecting a mantra, finding a quiet place, setting your intention, concentrating on your breath, repeating the mantra, staying focused and concluding the meditation. You can reap the advantages of mantra meditation, like improved mental clarity, improved concentration and heightened self-awareness, with constant effort. Try it out to see how this potent tool can change your life.

CHAPTER 9

CHANT YOUR FUCKIN' HEART OUT

CHANTING AND ITS IMPORTANCE IN MEDITATION

Chanting is one of the most important tools that we have available to us when we meditate, so let's talk about it now! Some of you may be thinking, "What does it mean to chant? Isn't that something that monks do in their cloisters all the time?" Friends, there is no need to be afraid! The practice of chanting is open to anyone and everyone; it is not limited to those who wear robes and have shaved heads.

So, what exactly is chanting? It is simple: Reciting a word, phrase, or sound over and over is an example of chanting. But, in case you were wondering, it's not just mindless repetition. Chanting is a powerful tool that can help you achieve a deeper meditative state. When you are chanting, it's almost as though someone is tapping you on the shoulder and saying, "Hey, pay attention!"

Now, I am aware that some of you might still have doubts about the practice of chanting. It's possible that you're thinking, "But my singing voice is terrible!" Good news: It is not necessary to have a strong singing voice to chant. The goal is to use your voice to produce a vibration that will help you quiet your mind and bring your thoughts back into focus. In addition, let's be honest: Nobody anticipates that you will compete on the next season of *American Idol*.

So, why is it that chanting plays such a significant role in meditation? When you chant, you produce a sound that travels through your entire body and creates vibrations. These vibrations have the potential to release tension and stress, which, in turn, can assist you in attaining a more relaxed state of mind. It's kind of like giving your brain a little head rub!

Increasing your focus and concentration is another benefit that can be gained from chanting. When you repeat a sound or phrase, it can help to clear your mind of other distractions. It's like having a reset button for your brain!

Perhaps the most important advantage of chanting is that it has the power to connect you to something that is more significant than yourself. The act of chanting can help bring about feelings of tranquility and comfort, regardless of whether you are chanting a holy word or simply repeating a mantra. It serves as a gentle prompt to keep in mind that you are an integral component of something larger than yourself, like a higher power, great spirit or the universe.

So, there you have it, folks! Chanting is a simple yet powerful tool that can help to deepen your meditation practice. Remember that chanting is not about being perfect, especially if you are still feeling a little unsure about what you are doing. The important thing is to be there and give it your best shot. So go ahead, give it a try! Who knows, maybe you'll find that singing your way to inner peace is exactly what you need.

THE POWER OF SOUND

Are you prepared to embark on an adventure into the bizarre world of sound and vibration? Strap in, because you're in for a ride that's not only going to be entertaining but also educational.

First, what, exactly, is sound? Sound is a type of energy that propagates through the atmosphere as a succession of vibrations. The sensation of hearing is triggered whenever those vibrations make contact with a person's eardrums. However, were you aware that those same vibrations can also affect our bodies and minds in some pretty strange ways?

Let's get the fundamentals out of the way first. It is common knowledge that certain types of music can have a significant effect on our feelings. But were you aware that there is scientific evidence to support that assertion? Dopamine is a chemical in our brains that makes us feel good, and one study that was published in *Nature Neuroscience* found that listening to music can cause our brains to produce more of this chemical. Another study found that listening to music that is happy and upbeat can actually improve our moods and make us feel happier. This research was published in the *Journal of Positive Psychology*.

Those positive vibrations can also be triggered by things other than music. Did you ever consider the possibility that the hum of a refrigerator or the buzz of a vibrator, or any other type of vibration, could have a significant impact on our health? In fact, the *Journal of Clinical and Diagnostic Research* reports that several studies have demonstrated that vibration therapy can assist in reducing pain and anxiety in fibromyalgia patients.

Chanting is another form of sound therapy that can be practiced if you're interested in taking a more spiritual approach to your treatment. The *International Journal of Environmental Research and Public Health* suggests that chanting can promote relaxation and help reduce stress. In addition, a study that was published in the journal *Evidence-Based Complementary and Alternative Medicine* discovered that singing bowls, which are those cool metal bowls that you might see in yoga studios, can help lower blood pressure and promote feelings of well-being in their users.

However, if you really want to go off the deep end, you could always give playing a didgeridoo a shot. Did you really just read that correctly? I'm talking about the long, tubular instrument that has been played by Indigenous Australians for thousands of years. Playing the didgeridoo can, according to a study that was published in *The BMJ*, help improve sleep apnea and reduce the amount of snoring that occurs during sleep.

It should now be clear that sound and vibration can produce some very peculiar effects on both our bodies and our minds. It doesn't matter if you're singing along to a didgeridoo or bopping your head to the beat of your favorite songs; what matters is that you're spreading positive energy.

Oh, you want to begin reciting some chants, do you? Fasten your seatbelt, sweetheart, because I'm about to take you on an exciting journey through the world of chanting for novices. There are a great many ways to get your chant on, ranging from the straightforward to the intricate, and we will investigate a few of these options.

To begin, let's look at the age-old "om." This chant consists of a single syllable, making it simple to learn and simple to articulate. Simply shut your eyes, take a deep breath, then exhale with a drawn-out "oooommmmmmm" sound. It's so easy that even your cat could figure it out, although maybe your cat sounds something more like "meowooooooooom."

The next chant to try is "om namah Shivaya." Although it is slightly lengthier than "om," it is still very simple to recall. The phrase literally translates to "I bow to Shiva," a powerful Hindu deity known for his strength. Therefore, if you're looking to unleash the superhero within you, this chant is exactly what you need.

Chant "Hare Krishna Hare Krishna, Krishna Krishna Hare Hare, Hare Rama Hare Rama, Rama Rama Hare Hare" if you're in the mood for something a little more daring. You can also try chanting "Hare Rama Hare Rama, Rama Rama Hare Hare." Although this one may be a little more difficult to chant, many people believe that this is the most effective mantra for cleansing the mind and bringing about an awakening of spiritual consciousness. When your friends at gatherings inquire as to what you've been up to recently, this chant is a fantastic opportunity to show off your accomplishments and leave them in awe.

You could try chanting "lokah samastah sukhino bhavantu," which translates to "May all beings everywhere be happy and free," if you're looking for something that will help you relax. This is a lovely sentiment that lends itself wonderfully to the development of compassion and empathy—and, honestly, all of our lives probably could use a little bit more of that kind of thing.

Last, but not least, there is the Sanskrit chant known as "om shanti shanti shanti," which translates to "peace." When you're feeling anxious or stressed out, focusing on this mantra can be very helpful. Be very careful not to nod off while chanting, as you may find that you wake up with a sore throat and drool all over your pillow.

These are a few chants to get you started on your path to finding peace within yourself. Keep in mind that chanting is similar to the exercise of a muscle; the more you do it, the stronger it will become. So, don't be afraid to practice and experiment with different chants until you find the one that resonates with you. Now, it's time to start chanting!

CHAPTER 10

MUDRAS FOR FUCKERS— HAND GESTURES 101

MEDITATION AND OTHER SPIRITUAL PRACTICES HAVE MADE USE OF MUDRAS, which are hand gestures, dating back thousands of years. It is believed that they originated in ancient India and have been utilized in the religious practices of Jainism, Buddhism and Hinduism at various times. It is believed that mudras have a powerful effect on both the mind and the body, and they have been utilized to promote physical as well as emotional well-being. Scientific research supports this as studies have found that practicing mudras can have various health benefits. For example, a 2017 study published in the *Journal of Alternative and Complementary Medicine* found that practicing a mudra called gyan mudra for 30 minutes daily for 8 weeks reduced anxiety and improved brain function in healthy adults.

HOW TO USE MUDRAS: TECHNIQUES FOR INCORPORATING MUDRAS INTO YOUR PRACTICE

There are many different approaches you can take to integrate mudras into your meditation routine, so you have plenty of options. You can do them while practicing seated meditation, or you can incorporate them into various yoga postures. In addition, you can use them while going about your daily activities like working or cooking. It is essential that you find a position that is comfortable for you and that you maintain the mudra for at least a few minutes, or for a longer period of time if that is what you prefer.

Focus on the breath whenever you are working with mudras as part of your practice. Your inhalation and exhalation should be slow and even, and you should bring your attention to the feeling that the breath creates in your body. This helps establish a connection between the physical and mental aspects of the practice, which ultimately results in a heightened sense of relaxation and inner tranquility.

If you want to get the most out of your meditation practice, familiarize yourself with mudras and try to incorporate them into your routine on a regular basis. Experiment with a variety of mudras to find the one that serves you in the most beneficial way, and then incorporate that mudra into your regular practice. Again, remember to focus on your breath and to maintain the mudra for at least a few minutes.

THREE MUDRAS FOR BEGINNERS

1.   Añjali mudra: This is a simple gesture of joining the palms of your hands together in front of the chest in a prayer-like position. It symbolizes the union of body, mind and spirit.

2.   Gyan mudra: This mudra involves touching the tip of the index finger to the tip of the thumb, while keeping the other three fingers straight. It is said to improve focus and concentration.

3. Prana mudra: This mudra involves covering the tips of the little finger and ring finger with the pad of the thumb. Extend the index and middle fingers. It is said to increase energy levels and vitality.

CHAPTER 11

GET YOUR MIND RIGHT— REPROGRAMMING WITH MEDITATION

THE POWER OF THE SUBCONSCIOUS MIND

Ah, yes, the subconscious mind, that mysterious underworld of our thoughts and emotions that we believed we had under control all along. However, it turns out that it is not the puppet at all; rather, it's the real puppet master, and it is the one pulling the strings and forcing us to do its bidding without us even realizing.

Studies have shown that our conscious minds are only responsible for 5 percent of our behavior and decision making, whereas our subconscious minds are responsible for 95 percent of our actions and choices (see *The Power of Your Subconscious Mind* by Dr. Joseph Murphy for more on this topic). This suggests that you need to rethink the assumption that you are always in charge and making your own decisions, my friend.

In fact, the power of the subconscious mind is such that it is capable of swaying our conscious beliefs and feelings without our awareness. Similar to how a magician can make you see things that aren't actually there, the subconscious has the ability to influence our perception of reality and the attitudes that we hold.

For instance, studies have shown that even if we are not consciously aware of subliminal messages, they can still influence our behavior and attitudes in significant ways. You now know who to blame the next time you find yourself reaching for that extra slice of pizza or experiencing a sudden urge to dance like nobody is watching: your subconscious mind!

The subconscious mind functions much like a secret agent, penetrating our conscious thoughts and deliberations to carry out its own covert objectives. Therefore, it is time to reclaim your power and initiate the process of reprogramming your subconscious mind to work *for you* rather than against you.

SUBCONSCIOUS REPROGRAMMING

Reprogramming your subconscious is similar to performing a software update on your brain. You can think of it as a way to upgrade your internal operating system and get rid of negative thought patterns and limiting beliefs that are preventing you from moving forward.

Think of the subconscious mind as the information technology department of your brain. It is in charge of managing all of your routine behaviors and responses that are triggered automatically. And just like any other IT department, it can occasionally become bogged down with outmoded beliefs and destructive thought patterns that simply aren't serving you any longer.

So, to get rid of these bugs, what do you do? Here is where reprogramming your subconscious comes into play! You can change these limiting beliefs and negative thought patterns using a variety of techniques, such as affirmations, visualization and hypnotherapy. This will allow you to replace them with beliefs and thought patterns that are brand new, positive and empowering.

Think of it as removing an outdated application with known bugs and replacing it with a brand-new version that functions properly. You will discover that you are able to reach your full potential and live a life that is happier and more fulfilling after you upgrade your subconscious.

Good, then let's get started on rewriting the script in your subconscious mind! Here are some steps for beginners:

1. Identify limiting beliefs: The first step to reprogramming your subconscious mind is to identify any limiting beliefs that may be holding you back. These could be negative thoughts or bouts of self-talk that prevent you from reaching your full potential. Write a list of these limiting beliefs and consider where they may have originated.

2. Affirm positive beliefs: Replace your limiting beliefs with positive, empowering affirmations. Write down affirmations that counteract your limiting beliefs and repeat them to yourself daily, especially when you find yourself thinking negatively.

3. Visualize your desired outcome: Visualization is a powerful tool for reprogramming your subconscious mind. Close your eyes and, as vividly as possible, imagine yourself achieving your desired outcome, complete with sights, sounds and emotions. Repeat this process daily, and you will start to believe in your ability to achieve your goals.

4. Engage in self-reflection: Take time each day to reflect on your thoughts, emotions and behaviors. Ask yourself what is driving your thoughts and behaviors, and what beliefs or experiences may be influencing them. This will help you become more self-aware and identify any areas where you may need to reprogram your subconscious mind.

5. Surround yourself with positivity: Populate your environment with positive people, music, books and other forms of media that support your desired outcome. This will help reinforce your positive affirmations and create a supportive environment for reprogramming your subconscious mind.

6. Practice gratitude: Focusing on the things you are grateful for can help shift your perspective and reprogram your subconscious mind. Start each day by listing a few things you are grateful for, and make a habit of noticing and appreciating the positive things in your life.

The strength of your subconscious mind is something that can't be disregarded. The bulk of your actions and choices are due to your subconscious, and its impact may be felt in a variety of facets of our lives. But, by reprogramming your subconscious brain, you can free yourself from the limiting beliefs and destructive thought patterns that may be preventing you from realizing your full potential. If you follow the procedures outlined above, you will be able to improve your internal operating system and begin leading a life that is happier and more rewarding. Keep in mind that the power to take control of your unconscious mind and create the life you have always dreamed of living is in your own hands.

CHAPTER 12

MANIFESTING YOUR DREAMS—LET'S GET THIS SHIT DONE

THE PROCESS OF BRINGING SOMETHING INTO THE PHYSICAL WORLD by employing optimistic thoughts and deeds is referred to as manifestation. The central tenet of this philosophy is that you can bring about the fulfillment of your goals and aspirations simply by concentrating on what it is that you want and imagining that it is already taking place in your life. Because it enables you to still your mind and concentrate on what you want to bring into existence, meditation is a potent instrument for manifestation.

THE RETICULAR ACTIVATING SYSTEM

Let me introduce you to the reticular activating system, or as we call it in the neuroscience community, the RAS. It's the gatekeeper of your consciousness. The RAS is the brain's equivalent of a ringmaster, determining which thoughts and activities take center stage and which are consigned to the sidelines. Basically, it's the part of your brain that decides which of the countless bits of data your senses constantly bombard it with is worth your attention.

So, why is the RAS so crucial? Well, consider this: If you were constantly required to pay attention to everything going on around you, your brain would be so overloaded that you would be unable to function. You would be running around like a crazy person on Red Bull, never pausing to catch your breath.

Fortunately, help arrived in the form of the RAS. Think of it as a mini-traffic officer stationed in your brain, whose job it is to evaluate all incoming inputs and give the green light (or the red) to the ones that are most important (or not important). The RAS allows you to ignore your irritating coworker yet perk up at the mere mention of pizza.

The RAS enjoys a good slice of pizza as much as the next person. In fact, it often uses its influence to make you forget about your responsibilities in favor of eating pizza. For this reason, you can find yourself thinking about pizza during a serious business meeting or academic lecture. All the RAS is doing is ensuring that you focus on what really matters.

But the RAS, like any good ringmaster, can be overzealous at times. Like a grating tune that won't leave your brain, it may determine that certain information needs to be hammered home at every opportunity. Alternately, it could become preoccupied by a dazzling object and fail to notice what it should really be focused on.

Hey, I guess that's the cost of the RAS doing its job so well. What is the cost? Sometimes paying attention to things that don't matter. The RAS does a terrific job of making sure the show goes on without a hitch and that you're paying attention to the details that matter most. So, the next time you're in the middle of a meeting and suddenly have a yearning for pizza, just nod at your RAS and realize it took control again. I mean, pizza is wonderful, but maybe let's not think about it in the middle of a meeting. Focus, fucker.

What you seek, you find. The RAS is great for finding what you're looking for so ask yourself: what do I want today? What am I seeking? If it's pizza, great, but maybe it's releasing fucks today. And if so, you'll find all the ways you can release your fucks in a single day.

FOCUS

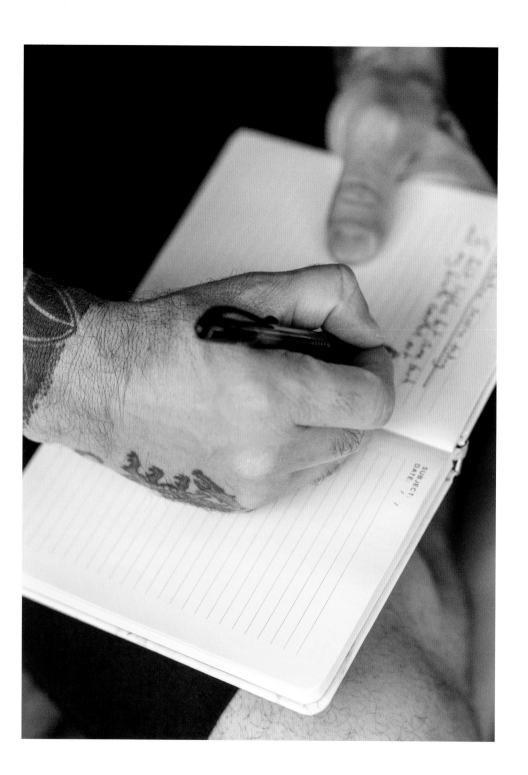

SETTING INTENTIONS, FOR FUCK'S SAKE

Intention setting is an essential component of the process of manifestation because it enables you to gain clarity over what it is that you want to attract into your life and aligns your thoughts, feelings and deeds with the result that you want to experience. The following are some steps that can assist you in effectively setting intentions for their manifestation:

1. Get clear on what you want. Take some time to reflect on what it is that you truly want to manifest. Be specific and focus on what you want to experience, rather than what you don't want.

2. Write down your intentions in a clear, concise and positive manner. This will help you clarify your thoughts and make them more concrete.

3. Focus on the feeling you want to experience, rather than just the outcome. For example, instead of simply saying, "I want a new car," say, "I want to feel the freedom and joy of driving a new car."

4. Make them achievable. Be sure your intentions are achievable and within your control. Focus on what you can do and what you have control over, rather than external factors outside of your control.

5. Align your thoughts, feelings and actions with your desired outcome. This means focusing on positive thoughts and emotions, taking action toward your goals and being consistent in your efforts.

6.   Review and adjust your intentions regularly. Remember, manifestation is a continuous process and your intentions may change as you grow and evolve.

By following these steps and setting clear, achievable and aligned intentions, you can bring more of what you want into your life and manifest your desires.

VISUALIZATION TECHNIQUES

Visualization is a powerful tool for the process of manifestation because it enables you to bring your desires and goals to life in your mind and aligns your thoughts, feelings and actions with your desired outcome. The following are some of the steps that can assist you in using visualization as a tool for manifestation:

1.   Get clear on what you want. Just like setting intentions, take some time to reflect on what it is that you truly want to manifest. Be specific and focus on exactly what you want to experience, rather than what you don't want.

2.   Close your eyes and relax. Find a quiet place where you won't be disturbed, close your eyes and take a few deep breaths to relax your mind and body.

3.   Create a vivid image in your mind. Using your imagination, create a vivid image in your mind of what it would look, feel and sound like if your desired outcome was already a reality. Use all of your senses to make the experience as real and vivid as possible.

4. Focus on the feeling, rather than just the outcome. For example, imagine your dream house. Imagine every single detail of your dream house. What sounds do you hear? How does it smell? What furniture is in your house? What is the temperature? Use all your senses to visualize your dream house and act like you are already inside. See it and feel it as if it actually exists, putting all your emotions into it. REALLY FEEL IT.

5. Make visualization a daily habit and spend a few minutes each day envisioning your desired outcome. The more often you visualize, the more likely you are to bring your desired outcome to life.

6. Affirm your desired outcome. Combine visualization with affirmations by repeating positive affirmations while you visualize. This helps to reinforce the positive message and align your thoughts, feelings and actions with your desired outcome.

Meditation is an efficient method for bringing one's goals to reality through the use of positive thoughts and deeds, which is an essential component in the process known as manifestation. The RAS plays a significant role in selecting the thoughts and actions that are allowed to occupy the forefront of your mind. In order to make clear intentions, you need to first consider what it is that you wish to bring into existence, then write down intentions that are positive and attainable, then concentrate on the sensation that you wish to feel. Visualizing is a great tool in the process because you can hijack your RAS to positive outcomes. Hijack your RAS to manifest the life you want. You may bring what you want into your life and manifest your wishes if you make use of these tactics and periodically assess and change your intentions.

CHAPTER 13

IT'S JUST FUCKIN' MEDITATION—YOU GOT THIS!

YOU ARE MAKING A SIGNIFICANT COMMITMENT TO YOUR OWN INNER CALM AND WELL-BEING when you make meditation a consistent part of your daily routine. When you practice mindfulness, there will be times when you feel as if you are a seasoned Zen master, and other times when you will feel as if you are an unrefined novice practicing for the first time. It is important to keep in mind that even if you are unable to maintain your meditation practice for some reason, the world will not stop; thus, give yourself permission to simply be there and enjoy the experience.

The practice of meditation offers benefits that are similar to those gained from successful long-term relationships. Both need a significant investment of time, in addition to dedication and hard work. Just as you might with a relationship, it's important to get yourself mentally ready for the ups and downs that come with meditation. As you might if you found yourself in the middle of an argument with your partner, keep in mind that the "disagreement" is not with meditation but rather with your thoughts that are roaming. Enjoy the way your thoughts come to you naturally and refuse to see this as a deficiency or a weakness.

Don't put undue pressure on yourself by striving for perfection. Scarcely a single person alive today can credibly assert that they are perfect, not even the person whose Instagram account you follow because they always seem to have their life together. It's much more likely that they're just really good at covering up their shortcomings. So, be kind to yourself and strive more toward improvement than perfection.

You won't be able to fully understand how much you've improved over the years unless you keep a record of your achievements. Since you started meditating, you may have noticed a surprising level of personal development. And even if you haven't grown at all, at least you're gaining a lot of experience, which is a good thing.

Those who are good at meditation typically have the traits of patience and empathy. If you find it difficult to concentrate or if you don't have any spontaneous epiphanies regarding your spirituality, try not to be too hard on yourself. Make an effort to be patient with yourself and acknowledge that this is a challenging task. Despite this, you should keep trying. If you just stay at it, over time it will become less difficult for you.

Remember that there is no reason to be concerned about meditating: It is completely safe. There is no shame in acknowledging that you did something wrong. What is outside your awareness is outside your control. When you become aware of something, you have the power to make a conscious choice to change. Your awareness is your greatest power and meditation allows you to become more and more aware. Finally, it is important to enjoy the process and to have fun with the journey. Meditation can be a great way to de-stress and stay present in the moment.

Dear friends who have been following along on this adventure with me, we have now arrived at our destination. We have discussed the ins and outs of meditation as well as the many factors that contribute to the difficulty of achieving inner stillness and peace on your own. But let us not forget that laughter is the best medicine, and that having a sense of humor is sometimes the best way to handle the challenges we face in life. For example, when I make a mistake leading a guided meditation or yoga class what gets me out of self-pity is just to laugh about it, even if I don't want to laugh. Fuckups happen. We aren't perfect. It's not that serious, so why not laugh about it? Try it out next time you fuck up. Just fake laugh out loud and see if you feel better.

Now, as we come to the end of this book, remember that the objective of meditation is not only to sit in stillness, but rather to achieve peace and harmony within yourself. Maintain a humorous approach toward your practice, and don't be overly critical of yourself if you do not always reach your goals.

Hence, the next time your meditation session is disrupted by a raucous neighbor, a ringing phone or a noisy appliance in the house, take a few deep breaths, let out a hearty chuckle and keep in mind that you are not the only person who has experienced these disruptions to your practice.

I sincerely hope that you were able to get some useful information and new perspectives from this book that will help you overcome the obstacles that arise during meditation and that you are able to continue reaping the numerous rewards this practice has to offer.

In the end, it all comes down to figuring out what works best for you and incorporating meditation into your daily routine in a consistent manner. I want to wish you the best of luck on your path to finding inner stillness and peace, regardless of whether you are an experienced meditator or you are just beginning. And remember, it's just fuckin' meditation. Don't take yourself so seriously.

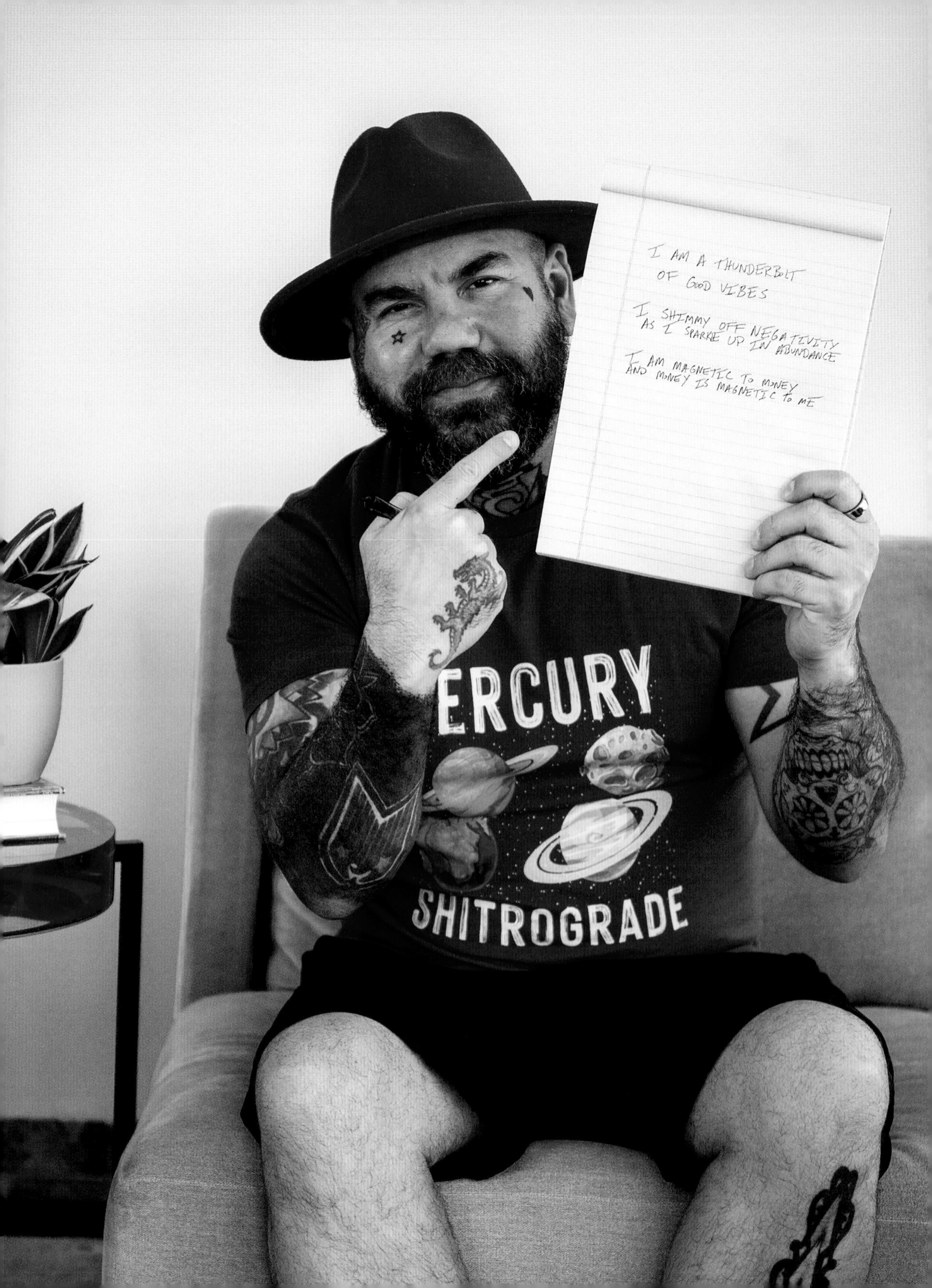
I AM A THUNDERBOLT
OF GOOD VIBES
I SHIMMY OFF NEGATIVITY
AS I SPARKLE UP IN ABUNDANCE
I AM MAGNETIC TO MONEY
AND MONEY IS MAGNETIC TO ME
ERCURY
SHITROGRADE

ACKNOWLEDGEMENTS

I would like to thank my parents Georg and Maxine, my brother Brandon, my amazing photographer Nicole, editor Marissa, my good friend Pratik, all my followers and fans, and Page Street Publishing for the support in writing this book. I couldn't have done it without you.

ABOUT THE AUTHOR

Yogi Bryan's goal is to help the world release 100 billion fucks.

He has a hypnotherapist certification from the San Diego Hypnosis Institute, is a neuro-linguistic programmer (NLP), an E-RYT 200 yoga instructor and a Yoga Alliance Continuing Education Provider (YACEP®). His *Relax with Yogi Bryan* meditation podcast has several million plays.

It all started from creating an Instagram page to make fun of yoga. Yogi Bryan loves to make the yoga and spiritual community laugh. He noticed people were very competitive and took their practice so seriously. "It's just fuckin' yoga," he thought. People need to relax and have fun on their yoga and meditation journey. Life is too short to be so intense. Bryan was inspired to create a space for the community where they could laugh while they practice because laughter is the best medicine.

Shortly after starting his yoga journey, Bryan began a consistent meditation practice. He challenged himself to meditate every single day for 90 days, and he hasn't stopped since.

The deeper Bryan went into his meditation practice, the more he realized the power of the subconscious mind. While he slept, Bryan continuously listened to hypnotic affirmations. Soon Bryan naturally and intuitively reprogrammed his subconscious mind with love, gratitude and abundance because he believes the subconscious mind is a powerful friend.

Bryan helps people just like you find their truth, gain confidence and release fucks.

INHALE:
RELAX THE BUTTCHEEKS
EXHALE:
RELEASE THE BUTTHEADS

SOURCES

Abbott, Ryan, and Helen Lavretsky. "Tai Chi and Qigong for the Treatment and Prevention of Mental Disorders." *Psychiatric Clinics of North America* 36, no, 1 (2013): 109–19. https://doi.org/10.1016/j.psc.2013.01.011

Álvarez-Pérez, Yolanda, Amado Rivero-Santana, Lilisbeth Perestelo-Pérez, Andrea Duarte-Díaz, Vanesa Ramos-García, Ana Toledo-Chávarri, Alexandra Torres-Castaño, et al. "Effectiveness of Mantra-Based Meditation on Mental Health: A Systematic Review and Meta-Analysis." *International Journal of Environmental Research and Public Health* 19, no. 6 (2020). https://doi.org/10.3390/ijerph19063380

Black, David S., Gillian A. O'Reilly, Richard Olmstead, Elizabeth C. Breen, and Michael R. Irwin. "Mindfulness Meditation and Improvement in Sleep Quality and Daytime Impairment among Older Adults with Sleep Disturbances: A Randomized Clinical Trial." *JAMA Internal Medicine* 175, no. 4 (2015): 494–501.

Buric, Ivana, Miguel Farias, Jonathan Jong, Christopher Mee, and Inti A. Brazil. "What Is the Molecular Signature of Mind–Body Interventions? A Systematic Review of Gene Expression Changes Induced by Meditation and Related Practices." *Frontiers in Immunology* 8 (2017). https://doi.org/10.3389/fimmu.2017.00670

Clark, David A., and Aaron T. Beck. "Cognitive Theory and Therapy of Anxiety and Depression: Convergence with Neurobiological Findings." *Trends in Cognitive Sciences* 14, no. 9 (2010): 418–24. https://doi.org/10.1016/j.tics.2010.06.007

Dhabhar, Firdaus S. "Effects of Stress on Immune Function: The Good, the Bad, and the Beautiful." *Immunologic Research* 58, no. 2–3 (2014): 193-210.

Edenfield, Teresa M., and Sy Atezaz Saaed. "An Update on Mindfulness Meditation as a Self-Help Treatment for Anxiety and Depression." *Psychology Research and Behavior Management* 5 (2012): 131–41.

Epel, E. S., E. Puterman, J. Lin, E. H. Blackburn, P. Y. Lum, N. D. Beckmann, J. Zhu, et al. "Meditation and Vacation Effects Have an Impact on Disease-Associated Molecular Phenotypes." *Translational Psychiatry* 6, no. 8 (2016): e880.

Ferguson, Yuna L., and Kennon M. Sheldon. "Trying to Be Happier Really Can Work: Two Experimental Studies. *Journal of Positive Psychology* 8, no 1 (2013): 23–33. https://doi.org/10.1080/17439760.2012.747000

Ferris, Emma. "How Deep Breathing Techniques Can Boost Your Immune System." December 26, 2018. https://www.thebreatheffect.com/immune-system-breathing-techniques/#:~:text=The%20study%20looked%20at%20what's,-step%20in%20the%20right%20direction

Gale, Cheryl. "Negative Self Talk: What Is it and Why Does it Matter?" May 12, 2023. https://www.proactivehm.com.au/negative-self-talk-what-is-it-and-why-does-it-matter

Gardi, Concetta, Teresa Fazia, Blerta Stringa, and Fabio Giommi. "A Short Mindfulness Retreat Can Improve Biological Markers of Stress and Inflammation." *Psychoneuroendocrinology* 135 (2022). https://doi.org/10.1016/j.psyneuen.2021.105579

Goldsby, Tamara R., Michael E. Goldsby, Mary McWalters, and Paul J. Mills. "The Effect of Singing Bowl Sound Meditation on Mood, Tension, and Well-Being: An Observational Study." *Evidence-Based Complementary and Alternative Medicine* 22, no. 3 (2017): 401–6.

Goyal, Madhav, Sonal Singh, Erica M. S. Sibinga, Neda F. Gould, Anastasia Rowland-Seymour, Ritu Sharma, Zackary Berger, et al. "Meditation Programs for Psychological Stress and Well-being: A Systematic Review and Meta-Analysis." *JAMA Internal Medicine* 174, no. 3 (2014): 357–68.

Hagins, Marshall, Rebecca States, Terry Selfe, and Kim Innes. "Effectiveness of Yoga for Hypertension: Systematic Review and Meta-Analysis." *Evidence-Based Complementary and Alternative Medicine* 2013. https://doi.org/10.1155/2013/649836

Joshi, Meesha, and Shirley Telles. "A Nonrandom-ized Non-Naive Comparative Study of the Effects of *Kapalabhati* and Breath Awareness on Event-Related Potentials in Trained Yoga Practitioners." *Journal of Alternative and Complementary Medicine* 15, no 3 (2009): 281–5.

Kim, Do-Young, Soo-Hwa Hong, Seung-Hyeon Jang, So-Hyeon Park, Jung-Hee Noh, Jung-Mi Seok, Hyun-Jeong Jo, et al. "Systematic Review for the Medical Applications of Meditation in Randomized Controlled Trials." *International Journal of Environmental Research and Public Health* 19, no. 3 (2022). https://doi.org/10.3390/ijerph19031244

Kross, Ethan, Matthew Davidson, Jochen Weber, and Kevin Ochsner. "Coping with Emotions Past: The Neural Bases of Regulating Affect Associated with Negative Autobiographical Memories." *Biological Psychiatry* 65, no 5 (2008): 361–6. https://doi.org/10.1016/j.biopsych.2008.10.019

la Cour, Peter, and Marian Peterson. "Effects of Mindfulness Medicine on Chronic Pain: A Random-ized Controlled Trial." *Pain Medicine* 16, no. 4 (2015): 641–52. https://doi.org/10.1111/pme.12605

Mayo Clinic Staff. "Meditation: A Simple Fast Way to Reduce Stress." April 29, 2022. https://www.mayoclinic.org/tests-procedures/meditation/in-depth/meditation/art-20045858

McEwen, Bruce S. "Central Effects of Stress Hormones in Health and Disease: Understanding the Protective and Damaging Effects of Stress and Stress Mediators." *European Journal of Pharmacology* 583, no. 2–3 (2008): 174–85.

Moynihan, Jan A., Benjamin P. Chapman, Rafael Klorman, Michael S. Krasner, Paul R. Duber-stein, Kirk Warren Brown, and Nancy L. Talbot. "Mindfulness-Based Stress Reduction for Older Adults: Effects on Executive Function, Frontal Alpha Asymmetry and Immune Function." *Neuropsychobiology* 68, no, 1 (2013). https://doi.org/10.1159/000350949

Murphy, Joseph. *The Power of Your Subconscious Mind*. Radford, VA: Wilder Publications, 2007.

National Center for Complementary and Integra-tive Health. "Meditation and Mindfulness: What You Need to Know." May 12, 2023. U.S. Department of Health and Human Services. https://www.nccih.nih.gov/health/meditation-and-mindfulness-what-you-need-to-know

Porges, Stephen W. *The Polyvagal Theory: Neuro-physiological Foundations of Emotions, Attachment, Communication, and Self-Regulation*. New York: W.W. Norton & Company, 2011.

Puhan, Milo A., Alex Suarez, Christian Lo Cascia, Alfred Zahn, Markus Heitz, and Otta Braendli. "Didgeridoo Playing as Alternative Treatment for Obstructive Sleep Apnoea Syndrome: Randomised Controlled Trial." *The BMJ* 332, no. 7536 (2006): 266–70.

Rea, Shilo. "Neurobiological Changes Explain How Mindfulness Meditation Improves Health." February 4, 2016. Carnegie Mellon University. https://www.cmu.edu/news/stories/archives/2016/february/meditation-changes-brain.html

Ruch, Simon, Marc Alain Züst, and Katharina Henke. "Subliminal Messages Exert Long-Term Effects on Decision-Making." *Neuroscience of Consciousness* 2016, no. 1 (2016). https://doi.org/10.1093/nc/niw013

Salimpoor, Valorie N., Mitchel Benovoy, Kevin Larcher, Alain Dagher, and Robert J. Zatorre. "Anatomically Distinct Dopamine Release During Anticipation and Experience of Peak Emotion to Music." *Nature Neuroscience* 14, no. 11 (2011): 257–62.

Salleh, Mohd Razali. "Life Event, Stress and Illness." *Malaysian Journal of Medical Science* 15, no. 4 (2008): 9–18.

Sanada, Kenji, Jesus Montero-Marin, Marta Alda Díez, Montserrat Salas-Valero, María C. Pérez-Yus, Héctor Morillo, Marcelo M. P. Demarzo, et al. "Effects of Mindfulness-Based Interventions on Salivary Cortisol in Healthy Adults: A Meta-Analytical Review." *Frontiers in Physiology* 7 (2016): 471.

Sutton, Jeremy. "Mindful Walking and Walking Meditation: A Restorative Practice." July 15, 2020. PositivePsychology.com. https://positivepsychology.com/mindful-walking/

Veqar, Zubia, and Shagufta Imtiyaz. "Vibration Therapy in Management of Delayed Onset Muscle Soreness (DOMS)." *Journal of Clinical and Diagnostic Research* 8, no. 6 (2014). https://doi.org/10.7860/JCDR/2014/7323.4434

Villalba, Daniella K., Emily K. Lindsay, Anna L. Marsland, Carol M. Greco, Shinzen Young, Kirk Warren Brown, Joshua M. Smyth, et al. "Mindfulness Training and Systemic Low-Grade Inflammation in Stressed Community Adults: Evidence from Two Randomized Controlled Trials." *PLOS ONE*. https://doi.org/10.1371/journal.pone.0219120

Wayne, Peter M., Jacquelyn N. Walsh, Ruth E. Taylor-Piliae, Rebecca E. Wells, Kathryn V. Papp, Nancy J. Donovan, and Gloria Y. Yeh. "Effect of Tai Chi on Cognitive Performance in Older Adults: Systematic Review and Meta-Analysis." *Journal of the American Geriatrics Society* 62, no. 1 (2014): 25–39.

Wielgosz, Joseph, Simon B. Goldberg, Tammi R. A. Kral, John D. Dunne, and Richard J. Davidson. "Mindfulness Meditation and Psychopathology." *Annual Review of Clinical Psychology* 15 (2019): 285–316.

Yang, Kyeongra. "A Review of Yoga Programs for Four Leading Risk Factors of Chronic Diseases." *Evidence-Based Complementary and Alternative Medicine* 4, no. 4 (2007): 487–91.

Zaccaro, Andrea, Andrea Piarulli, Marco Laurino, Erika Garbella, Danilo Menicucci, Bruno Neri, and Angelo Gemignani. "How Breath-Control Can Change Your Life: A Systematic Review on Psycho-Physiological Correlates of Slow Breathing." *Frontiers in Human Neuroscience* 12 (2018). https://doi.org/10.3389/fnhum.2018.00353

Zeidan, Fadel, Susan K. Johnson, Nakia S. Gordon, and Paula Goolkasian. "Effects of Brief and Sham Mindfulness Meditation on Mood and Cardiovascular Variables." *Journal of Alternative and Complementary Medicine* 16, no 8 (2010): 867–73.

INDEX